BLOCKCHAIN BASICS

A NON-TECHNICAL INTRODUCTION IN 25 STEPS

Daniel Drescher

Apress®

Blockchain Basics: A Non-Technical Introduction in 25 Steps

Daniel Drescher
Frankfurt am Main, Germany

ISBN-13 (pbk): 978-1-4842-2603-2   ISBN-13 (electronic): 978-1-4842-2604-9
DOI 10.1007/978-1-4842-2604-9

Library of Congress Control Number: 2017936232

Managing Director: Welmoed Spahr
Editorial Director: Todd Green
Acquisitions Editor: Susan McDermott
Development Editor: Laura Berendson
Technical Reviewer: Laurence Kirk
Coordinating Editor: Rita Fernando
Copy Editor: Mary Bearden
Compositor: SPi Global
Indexer: SPi Global
Artist: SPi Global

Distributed to the book trade worldwide by Springer Science+Business Media New York, 233 Spring Street, 6th Floor, New York, NY 10013. Phone 1-800-SPRINGER, fax (201) 348-4505, e-mail orders-ny@springer-sbm.com, or visit www.springeronline.com. Apress Media, LLC is a California LLC and the sole member (owner) is Springer Science + Business Media Finance Inc (SSBM Finance Inc). SSBM Finance Inc is a **Delaware** corporation.

For information on translations, please e-mail rights@apress.com, or visit http://www.apress.com/rights-permissions.

Apress titles may be purchased in bulk for academic, corporate, or promotional use. eBook versions and licenses are also available for most titles. For more information, reference our Print and eBook Bulk Sales web page at http://www.apress.com/bulk-sales.

Any source code or other supplementary material referenced by the author in this book is available to readers on GitHub via the book's product page, located at www.apress.com/9781484226032. For more detailed information, please visit http://www.apress.com/source-code.

Apress Business: The Unbiased Source of Business Information

Apress business books provide essential information and practical advice, each written for practitioners by recognized experts. Busy managers and professionals in all areas of the business world—and at all levels of technical sophistication—look to our books for the actionable ideas and tools they need to solve problems, update and enhance their professional skills, make their work lives easier, and capitalize on opportunity.

Whatever the topic on the business spectrum—entrepreneurship, finance, sales, marketing, management, regulation, information technology, among others—Apress has been praised for providing the objective information and unbiased advice you need to excel in your daily work life. Our authors have no axes to grind; they understand they have one job only—to deliver up-to-date, accurate information simply, concisely, and with deep insight that addresses the real needs of our readers.

It is increasingly hard to find information—whether in the news media, on the Internet, and now all too often in books—that is even-handed and has your best interests at heart. We therefore hope that you enjoy this book, which has been carefully crafted to meet our standards of quality and unbiased coverage.

We are always interested in your feedback or ideas for new titles. Perhaps you'd even like to write a book yourself. Whatever the case, reach out to us at editorial@apress.com and an editor will respond swiftly. Incidentally, at the back of this book, you will find a list of useful related titles. Please visit us at www.apress.com to sign up for newsletters and discounts on future purchases.

The Apress Business Team

Contents

About the Author

Daniel Drescher is an experienced banking professional who has held positions in electronic security trading in several banks. His recent activities have focused on automation, machine learning, and big data in the context of security trading. Among others, Daniel holds a doctorate in econometrics from the Technical University of Berlin and an MSc in software engineering from the University of Oxford.

About the Technical Reviewer

Laurence Kirk who after a successful career writing low latency financial applications for the City of London, was captivated by the potential of distributed ledger technology. He moved to Oxford to study for his master's degree and set up Extropy.io, a consultancy working with start-ups to develop applications on the Ethereum platform. Passionate about distributed technology, he now works as a developer, evangelist, and educator about Ethereum.

Introduction

This introduction answers the most important question that every author has to answer: Why should anyone read this book? Or more specifically: Why should anyone read another book about the blockchain? Continue reading and you will learn why this book was written, what you can expect from this book, what you cannot expect from this book, for whom the book was written, and how the book is structured.

Why Another Book About the Blockchain?

The blockchain has received a lot of attention in the public discussion and in the media. Some enthusiasts claim that the blockchain is the biggest invention since the emergence of the Internet. Hence, a lot of books and articles have been written in the past few years about the blockchain. However, if you want to learn more about how the blockchain works, you may find yourself lost in a universe of books that either quickly skim over the technical details or that discuss the underlying technical concepts at a highly formal level. The former may leave you unsatisfied because they miss to explain the technical details necessary to understand and appreciate the blockchain, while the latter may leave you unsatisfied because they already require the knowledge you want to acquire.

This book fills the gap that exists between purely technical books about the blockchain, on the one hand, and the literature that is mostly concerned with specific applications or discussions about its expected economic impact or visions about its future, on the other hand.

This book was written because a conceptual understanding of the technical foundations of the blockchain is necessary in order to understand specific blockchain applications, evaluate business cases of blockchain startups, or follow the discussion about its expected economic impacts. Without an appreciation of the underlying concepts, it will be impossible to assess the value or the potential impact of the blockchain in general or understand the added value of specific blockchain applications. This book focuses on the underlying concepts of the blockchain since a lack of understanding of a new technology can lead to being carried away with the hype and being disappointed later on because of unrealistic unsubstantiated expectations.

This book teaches the concepts that make up the blockchain in a nontechnical fashion and in a concise and comprehensible way. It addresses the three big questions that arise when being introduced to a new technology: What is it? Why do we need it? How does it work?

What You Cannot Expect from This Book

The book is deliberately agnostic to the application of the blockchain. While cryptocurrencies in general and Bitcoin in particular are prominent applications of the blockchain, this book explains the blockchain as a general technology. This approach has been chosen in order to highlight generic concepts and technical patterns of the blockchain instead of focusing on a specific and narrow application case. Hence, this book is:

- Not a text specifically about Bitcoin or any other cryptocurrency

- Not a text solely about one specific blockchain application

- Not a text about proofing the mathematical foundations of the blockchain

- Not a text about programming a blockchain

- Not a text about the legal consequences and implications of the blockchain

- Not a text about the social, economic, or ethical impacts of the blockchain on our society or humankind in general

However, some of these points are addressed to some extent at appropriate points in this book.

What You Can Expect from This Book

This book explains the technical concepts of the blockchain such as transactions, hash values, cryptography, data structures, peer-to-peer systems, distributed systems, system integrity, and distributed consensus in a nontechnical fashion. The didactical approach of this book is based on four elements:

- Conversational style

- No mathematics and no formulas

- Incremental steps through the problem domain

- Use of metaphors and analogies

Conversational Style

This book is deliberately written in a conversational style. It does not use mathematical or computer science jargon in order to avoid any hurdle for nontechnical readers. However, the book introduces and explains the necessary terminology needed to join the discussion and to understand other publications about the blockchain.

No Mathematics and No Formulas

Major elements of the blockchain such as cryptography and algorithms are based on complex mathematical concepts, which in turn come with their own demanding and sometimes frightening mathematical notation and formulas. However, this book deliberately does not use any mathematical notation or formulas in order to avoid any unnecessary complexity or hurdle for nontechnical readers.

Incremental Steps Through the Problem Domain

The chapters in this book are called *steps* for a good reason. These steps form a learning path that incrementally builds the knowledge about the blockchain. The order of the steps was chosen carefully. They cover the fundamentals of software engineering, explain the terminology, point out the reason why the blockchain is needed, and explain the individual concepts that make up the blockchain as well as their interactions. Calling the individual chapters steps highlights their dependence and their didactical purpose. They form a logical sequence to be followed instead of being chapters that could be read independently.

Use of Metaphors and Analogies

Each step that introduces a new concept starts with a pictorial explanation by referring to a situation from real life. These metaphors serve four major purposes. First, they prepare the reader for introduction to a new technical concept. Second, by connecting a technical concept to an easy-to-understand real-world scenario, the metaphors reduce the mental hurdle to discover a new territory. Third, metaphors allow learning new concepts by similarities and analogies. Finally, metaphors provide rules of thumb for memorizing new concepts.

How This Book Is Organized

This book consists of 25 steps grouped into five major stages that all together form a learning path, which incrementally builds your knowledge of the blockchain. These steps cover some fundamentals of software engineering, explain the required terminology, point out the reasons why the blockchain is needed, explain the individual concepts that make up the blockchain as well as their interactions, consider applications of the blockchain, and mention areas of active development and research.

Stage I: Terminology and Technical Foundations

Steps 1 to 3 explain major concepts of software engineering and set the terminology necessary for understanding the succeeding steps. By the end of Step 3, you will have gained an overview of the fundamental concepts and an appreciation of the big picture in which the blockchain is located.

Stage II: Why the Blockchain Is Needed

Steps 4 to 7 explain why the blockchain is needed, what problem it solves, why solving this problem is important, and what potential the blockchain has. By the end of Step 7, you will have gained a good understanding of the problem domain in which the blockchain is located, the environment in which it provides the most value, and why it is needed in the first place.

Stage III: How the Blockchain Works

The third stage is the centerpiece of this book since it explains how the blockchain works internally. Steps 8 to 21 guide you through 15 distinct technical concepts that all together make up the blockchain. By the end of Step 21, you will have reached an understanding of all the major concepts of the blockchain, how they work in isolation, and how they interact in order to create the big machinery that is called the blockchain.

Stage IV: Limitations and How to Overcome Them

Steps 22 to 23 focus on major limitations of the blockchain, explain their reasons, and sketch possible ways to overcome them. By the end of Step 23, you will understand why the original idea of the blockchain as explained in the previous steps may not be suitable for large-scale commercial applications, what changes were made to overcome these limitations, and how these changes altered the properties of the blockchain.

Stage V: Using the Blockchain, Summary, and Outlook

Steps 24 and 25 consider how the blockchain can be used in real life and what questions should to be addressed when selecting a blockchain application. This stage also points out areas of active research and further development. By the end of Step 25, you will have gained a well-grounded understanding of the blockchain and you will be well prepared to read more advanced texts or to become an active part in the ongoing discussion about the blockchain.

Accompanying Material

The website www.blockchain-basics.com offers accompanying material for some of the steps of this book.

Terminology and Technical Foundations

This stage explains major concepts of software engineering and establishes a way to organize and standardize our communication about technology. This learning stage also introduces the concepts of software architecture and integrity and how they relate to the blockchain. By the end of this stage, you will have gained an understanding of the purpose of the blockchain and its potential.

Thinking in Layers and Aspects

Analyzing systems by separating them into layers and aspects

This step lays the foundation of our learning path through the blockchain by introducing a way to organize and standardize our communication about technology. This step explains how you can analyze a software system and why it is important to consider a software system as a composition of layers. Furthermore, this step illustrates what you can gain from considering different layers in a system and how this approach helps us to understand the blockchain. Finally, this step provides a short introduction to the concept of software integrity and highlights its importance.

© Daniel Drescher 2017
D. Drescher, *Blockchain Basics*, DOI 10.1007/978-1-4842-2604-9_1

The Metaphor

Do you have a mobile phone? I would guess yes, as most people now have at least one. How much do you know about the different wireless communication protocols that are used to send and receive data? How much do you know about electromagnetic waves that are the foundation of mobile communication? Well, most of us do not know very much about these details because it is not necessary to know them in order to use a mobile phone and most of us do not have the time to learn about them. We mentally separate the mobile phone into the parts we need to know and the parts that can be ignored or taken for granted.

This approach to technology is not restricted to mobile phones. We use it all the time when we learn how to use a new television set, a computer, a washing machine, and so forth. However, these mental partitions are highly individual since what is considered important and what is not depends on our individual preferences, the specific technology, and our goals and experiences. As a result, your mental partition of a mobile phone may differ from my mental partition of the same mobile phone. This typically leads to problems in communication in particular when I try to explain to you what you should know about a certain mobile phone. Hence, unifying the way of partitioning a system is the key point when teaching and discussing technology. This step explains how to partition or layer a system and hence sets the basis for our communication about the blockchain.

Layers of a Software System

The following two ways of partitioning a system are used throughout this book:

- Application vs. implementation
- Functional vs. nonfunctional aspects

Application vs. Implementation

Mentally separating the user's needs from the technical internals of a system leads to a separation of the application layer from the implementation layer. Everything that belongs to the application layer is concerned with the user's needs (e.g., listening to music, taking photos, or booking hotel rooms). Everything that belongs to the implementation layer is concerned with making these things happen (e.g., converting digital information into acoustic signals, recognizing the color of a pixel in a digital camera, or sending messages over the Internet to a booking system). Elements of the implementation layer are technical by nature and are considered a means to an end.

Functional vs. Nonfunctional Aspects

Distinguishing between what a system does and how it does what it does leads to the separation of functional and nonfunctional aspects. Examples of functional aspects are sending data over a network, playing music, taking photos, and manipulating individual pixels of a picture. Examples of nonfunctional aspects are a beautiful graphical user interface, fast-running software, and an ability to keep user data private and save. Other important nonfunctional aspects of a system are security and integrity. *Integrity* means that a system behaves as intended, and it involves many aspects such as security and correctness.[1] There is a nice way to remember the difference between functional and nonfunctional aspects of a system by referring to grammar usage in the English language: verbs describe actions or what is done, while adverbs describe how an action is done. For example, a person can walk quickly or slowly. In both cases, the action of "walk" is identical but how the action is performed differs. As a rule of thumb, one can say that functional aspects are similar to verbs, while nonfunctional aspects are similar to adverbs.

Considering Two Layers at the Same Time

Identifying functional and nonfunctional aspects as well as separating application and implementation layer can be done at the same time, which leads to a two-dimensional table. Table 1-1 illustrates the result of mentally layering a mobile phone in this way.

Table 1-1. Example of Mentally Layering a Mobile Phone

Layer	Functional Aspects	Nonfunctional Aspects
Application	Taking photos Making phone calls Sending e-mails Browsing the Internet Sending chat messages	The graphical user interface looks beautiful Easy to use Messages are sent fast
Implementation	Saving user data internally Making a connection to the nearest mobile connector Accessing pixels in the digital camera	Store data efficiently Saving energy Maintaining integrity Ensure user privacy

---

[1]Chung, Lawrence, et al. *Non-functional requirements in software engineering.* Vol. 5. New York: Springer Science & Business Media, 2012.

Table 1-1 may explain the visibility (or the lack of it) of specific elements of a system to its users. Functional aspects of the application layer are the most obvious elements of a system, because they serve obvious needs of the users. These elements are typically the ones users learn about. On the other hand, the nonfunctional aspects of the implementation layer are rarely seen as major elements of the system. They are typically taken for granted.

Integrity

Integrity is an important nonfunctional aspect of any software system. It has three major components[2]:

- *Data integrity*: The data used and maintained by the system are complete, correct, and free of contradictions.

- *Behavioral integrity*: The system behaves as intended and it is free of logical errors.

- *Security*: The system is able to restrict access to its data and functionality to authorized users only.

Most of us may take integrity of software systems for granted because most of the time we luckily interact with systems that keep their integrity. This is due to the fact that programmers and software engineers have invested a lot of time and effort into the development of systems to achieve and maintain integrity. As a result, we may be a bit spoiled when it comes to appreciating the work done by software engineers to create systems that maintain a high level of integrity. But our feelings may change as soon as we interact with a system that fails to do so. These are the occasions when you face a loss of data, illogical software behavior, or realize that strangers were able to access your private data. These are the occasions when your mobile phone, your computer, your e-mail software, your word processor, or your spreadsheet calculator make you angry and forget your good manners! On these occasions, we begin to realize that software integrity is a highly valuable commodity. Hence, it should not come as a surprise that software professionals spend a lot of their time working on this seemingly tiny nonfunctional aspect of the implementation layer.

---

[2] Boritz, J. Efrim. IS practitioners' views on core concepts of information integrity. *International Journal of Accounting Information Systems* 6.4 (2005): 260–279.

Outlook

This step provided an introduction to some general principles of software engineering. In particular, the concepts of integrity and functional vs. nonfunctional aspects as well as application vs. implementation of a software system were illustrated. Understanding these concepts will help you appreciate the wider scope in which the blockchain exists. The next step will present the bigger picture by using the concepts introduced in this step.

Summary

- Systems can be analyzed by separating them into:
    - Application and implementation layer
    - Functional and nonfunctional aspects

- The application layer focuses on the user's needs, while the implementation layer focuses on making things happen.

- Functional aspects focus on what is done, while nonfunctional aspects focus on how things are done.

- Most users are concerned with the functional aspects of the application layer of a system, while nonfunctional aspects of a system, in particular those of the implementation layer, are less visible to users.

- Integrity is an important nonfunctional aspect of any software system and it has three major elements:
    - Data integrity
    - Behavioral integrity
    - Security

- Most software failures, such as losses of data, illogical behavior, or strangers accessing one's private data, are the result of violated system integrity.

Seeing the Big Picture

Software architecture and its relation to the blockchain

This step not only provides the big picture in which the blockchain is located, but it also highlights its location within the big picture. In order to allow you to see the big picture, this step introduces the concept of software architecture and explains its relation to the concept of separating a system into layers and aspects. In order to help you recognize the location of the blockchain within the big picture, this step highlights the relationship between the blockchain and software architecture. Finally, this step points out the core purpose of the blockchain in just one sentence. Appreciating its purpose is a cornerstone in understanding the blockchain and understanding the course of the succeeding steps.

The Metaphor

Have you ever bought a car? Most of us have. Even if you have never bought a car, you probably know that cars are equipped with different types of engines (e.g., diesel, gasoline, or electric engine). This is an example of the process

© Daniel Drescher 2017
D. Drescher, *Blockchain Basics*, DOI 10.1007/978-1-4842-2604-9_2

of modularization, which is the result of applying the idea of layering to cars. Having the choice among different engines when buying a car can result in amazing differences in the vehicle. Two cars that look identical from the outside can differ dramatically with respect to the power of their engines and hence have very different driving performance. Additionally, your choice of the engine will have an impact on other characteristics of the car, like its price, its operational costs, the type of fuel consumed, the exhaust system, and the dimensions of the brakes. With this picture in mind, understanding the role of the blockchain within the big picture will be much easier.

A Payment System

Let's apply the concept of layering to a payment system. Table 2-1 shows some of the user's needs as well as some of the nonfunctional aspects of both the application and the implementation layers.

Table 2-1. Aspects and Layers of a Payment System

Layer	Functional Aspects	Nonfunctional Aspects
Application	Deposit money	The graphical user interface looks beautiful
	Withdraw money	Easy to use
	Transfer money	Transfer of money is done fast
	Monitor account balance	System has many participants
Implementation	?	Available 24 hours a day
		Fraud resistant
		Maintaining integrity
		Ensure user privacy

Have you spotted the question mark in that part of the table were you normally see information about the technology used to make the system work? This space was left blank on purpose. It is the place where you decide which "engine" should be used to run your system. The next section will tell you a bit more about the engine equivalent in software systems.

Two Types of Software Architecture

There are many ways to implement software systems. However, one of the fundamental decisions when implementing a system concerns its architecture, the way in which its components are organized and related to one another.

The two major architectural approaches for software systems are centralized and distributed.[1]

In centralized software systems, the components are located around and connected with one central component. In contrast, the components of distributed systems form a network of connected components without having any central element of coordination or control.

Figure 2-1 depicts these two contrary architectures. The circles in the figure represent system components, also called nodes, and the lines represent connections between them. At this point, it is not important to know the details of what these components do and what information is exchanged between the nodes. The important point is the existence of these two different ways of organizing software systems. On the left-hand side of Figure 2-1, a distributed architecture is illustrated where components are connected with one another without having a central element. It is important to see that none of the components is directly connected with all other components. However, all components are connected with one another at least indirectly. The right-hand side of Figure 2-1 illustrates a centralized architecture where each component is connected to one central component. The components are not connected with one another directly. They only have one direct connection to the central component.

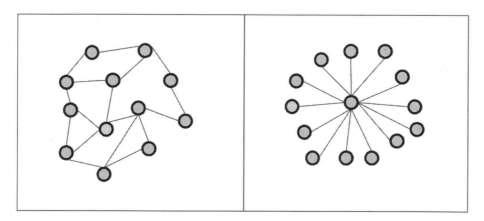

Figure 2-1. Distributed (left) vs. centralized (right) system architecture

---

[1]Tanenbaum, Andrew S., and Maarten Van Steen. *Distributed systems: principles and paradigms.* Upper Saddle River, NJ: Pearson Prentice Hall, 2007.

The Advantages of Distributed Systems

The major advantages of a distributed system over single computers are[2]:

- Higher computing power
- Cost reduction
- Higher reliability
- Ability to grow naturally

Higher Computing Power

The computing power of a distributed system is the result of combining the computing power of all connected computers. Hence, distributed systems typically have more computing power than each individual computer. This has been proven true even when comparing distributed systems comprised of computers of relatively low computing power with isolated super computers.

Cost Reduction

The price of mainstream computers, memory, disk space, and networking equipment has fallen dramatically during the past 20 years. Since distributed systems consist of many computers, the initial costs of distributed systems are higher than the initial costs of individual computers. However, the costs of creating, maintaining, and operating a super computer are still much higher than the costs of creating, maintaining, and operating a distributed system. This is particularly true since replacing individual computers of a distributed system can be done with no significant overall system impact.

Higher Reliability

The increased reliability of a distributed system is based on the fact that the whole network of computers can continue operating even when individual machines crash. A distributed system does not have a single point of failure. If one element fails, the remaining elements can take over. Hence, a single super computer typically has a lower reliability than a distributed system.

---

[2]Tanenbaum, Andrew S., and Maarten Van. Steen. *Distributed systems: principles and paradigms*. Upper Saddle River, NJ: Pearson Prentice Hall, 2007.

Ability to Grow Naturally

The computing power of a distributed system is the result of the aggregated computing power of its constituents. One can increase the computing power of the whole system by connecting additional computers with the system. As a result, the computing power of the whole system can be increased incrementally on a fine-grained scale. This supports the way in which the demand for computing power increases in many organizations. The incremental growth of distributed systems is in contrast to the growth of the computing power of individual computers. Individual computers provide identical power until they are replaced by a more powerful computer. This results in a discontinuous growth of computing power, which is only rarely appreciated by the consumers of computing services.

The Disadvantages of Distributed Systems

The disadvantages of distributed systems compared to single computers are:

- Coordination overhead
- Communication overhead
- Dependency on networks
- Higher program complexity
- Security issues

Coordination Overhead

Distributed systems do not have central entities that coordinate their members. Hence, the coordination must be done by the members of the system themselves. Coordinating work among coworkers in a distributed system is challenging and costs effort and computing power that cannot be spent on the genuine computing task, hence, the term coordination overhead.

Communication Overhead

Coordination requires communication. Hence, the computers that form a distributed system have to communicate with one another. This requires the existence of a communication protocol and the sending, receiving, and processing of messages, which in turn costs effort and computing power that cannot be spend on the genuine computing task, hence, the term communication overhead.

Dependencies on Networks

Any kind of communication requires a medium. The medium is responsible for transferring information between the entities communicating with one another. Computers in distributed systems communicate by means of messages passed through a network. Networks have their own challenges and adversities, which in turn impact the communication and coordination among computers that form a distributed system. However, without any network, there will be no distributed system, no communication, and therefore no coordination among the nodes, thus the dependency on networks.

Higher Program Complexity

Solving a computation problem involves writing programs and software. Due to the disadvantages mentioned previously, any software in a distributed system has to solve additional problems such as coordination, communication, and utilizing of networks. This increases the complexity of the software.

Security Issues

Communication over a network means sending and sharing data that are critical for the genuine computing task. However, sending information through a network implies security concerns as untrustworthy entities may misuse the network in order to access and exploit information. Hence, any distributed system has to address security concerns. The less restricted the access to the network over which the distributed nodes communicate is, the higher the security concerns are for the distributed system.

Distributed Peer-to-Peer Systems

Peer-to-peer networks are a special kind of distributed systems. They consist of individual computers (also called nodes), which make their computational resources (e.g., processing power, storage capacity, data or network bandwidth) directly available to all other members of the network without having any central point of coordination. The nodes in the network are equal concerning their rights and roles in the system. Furthermore, all of them are both suppliers and consumers of resources.

Peer-to-peer systems have interesting applications such as file sharing, content distribution, and privacy protection. Most of these applications utilize a simple but powerful idea: turning the computers of the users into nodes that make up the whole distributed system. As a result, the more users or customers use the software, the larger and more powerful the system becomes. This idea, its consequences, and it challenges are discussed in the following steps.

Mixing Centralized and Distributed Systems

Centralized and distributed systems are architectural antipodes. Technical antipodes have always inspired engineers to create hybrid systems that inherit the strength of their parents. Centralized and distributed systems are no exception to this. There are two archetypical ways of combining these antipodes, and they need to be understood since they will become important when learning about blockchain applications in the real world. They are centrality within a distributed system and the distributed system inside the center.

The graphic on the left-hand side of Figure 2-2 illustrates an architecture that establishes a central component within a distributed system. On first glance, the components seem to form a distributed system. However, all of the circles are connected with the larger circle located in the middle. Hence, such a system only appears to be distributed on a superficial view, but it is a centralized system in reality.

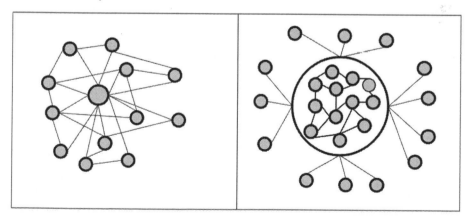

Figure 2-2. Mixing distributed with centralized architecture

The graph on the right-hand side of Figure 2-2 illustrates the opposite approach. Such a system appears to be a centralized system on first glance, because all the circles in the periphery only have one direct connection to a large central component. However, the central component contains a distributed system inside. The components in the periphery may not even be aware of the distributed system that lives within the central component.

What these two approaches have in common is that it is hard to determine their true nature. Are they distributed or centralized? It may not be necessary to give these architectures unique names. However, it is important to point out their dual nature. This is particularly important because it may not be easy to spot the centrality or the distributed nature within them. I will come back to this point later when I discuss the way the blockchain is commercialized.

Identifying Distributed Systems

The emergence of hybrid architectures makes it hard to identify distributed systems clearly. Formulating a generally accepted definition of distributed systems is beyond the scope of this book. However, for the course of this book it is important to have an idea of what a distributed system is and how it differs from other software systems. If you are in doubt whether or not a system is distributed, look for a single component (e.g., a database, a name or user registry, a login or logoff component, or an emergency switch-off button) that could terminate the whole system. If you find such a component, the system under consideration is not distributed.

■ Note   If one single component exists, e.g., a single switch-off button that can bring down the whole system, then the system is not distributed.

The Purpose of the Blockchain

When designing a software system, one can choose which architectural style will be used, similar to choosing an engine for a car. The architectural decision can be done independently from the functional aspects of the application layer. As a result, one can create distributed as well as centralized systems with identical functionality on the application layer. The architecture is only a means to an end when it comes to implementing a system. Hence, a payment system, as was proposed in Table 2-1, can be implemented as a distributed or centralized system.

Each of the two architectural concepts has its own advantages and disadvantages and their own specific way of doing things. Choosing a specific architecture has consequences on how you will achieve the functional and nonfunctional aspects of a system. In particular, both architectural concepts have very different approaches to ensure integrity. And this is the point where the blockchain enters the picture. The blockchain is a tool for achieving integrity in distributed software systems. Hence, it can be seen as a tool to achieve a nonfunctional aspect of the implementation layer.

Note   The purpose of the blockchain is to achieve and maintain integrity in distributed systems.

Outlook

Achieving integrity in a distributed system is very technical and it may sound a bit boring. However, the question that makes this achievement exciting for many people depends on what the distributed system will do and what kind of centralized system it replaces. The next step explains how a peer-to-peer system has changed our world and why the blockchain as a tool for achieving integrity in distributed software systems has the potential to change the world too.

Summary

- The architecture of a software system determines how its components are organized and related to one another.

- Centralized and distributed software architectures can be seen as antipodes.

- A distributed system consists of a number of independent computers that cooperate with one another by using a communication medium in order to achieve a specific objective without having any centralized element of control or coordination.

- As a rule of thumb, one can state that as soon as a system has a single component that could bring down the whole system it is not distributed, regardless of how complex its architecture looks.

- The blockchain is part of the implementation layer of a distributed software system.

- The purpose of the blockchain is to ensure a specific nonfunctional aspect of a distributed software system that is: achieving and maintaining its integrity.

Recognizing the Potential

How peer-to-peer systems may change the world

This step deepens our understanding of the purpose of the blockchain by considering a specific kind of distributed system: the peer-to-peer system. As a result, this step will help you understanding why there is so much excitement about the blockchain among technologists and business professionals alike. This step also points out the major area of application in which the blockchain is expected to provide the most value. Additionally, this step discusses some consequences of peer-to-peer systems in the real world.

The Metaphor

Can you remember the last time you bought a CD for yourself in a music store or in a department store? Most people have not bought actual CDs for a long time now, because the music industry went through a dramatic change. Nowadays, people download individual songs from music portals, share mp3 files among friends, or use music streams on their mobile devices instead of buying CDs. This change started with the emergence of a piece of software

© Daniel Drescher 2017
D. Drescher, *Blockchain Basics*, DOI 10.1007/978-1-4842-2604-9_3

that allowed people to share their music files with one another. But what was so special about that software? This is what one of its inventors had to say about this:

> This system, what's most interesting about it is, you're interacting with peers, you're exchanging information with a person down the street.
>
> —Shawn Fanning, cofounder of Napster

What Fanning and his coworkers invented was a peer-to-peer system for sharing music. Back in the late 1990s, this software ushered in a new era for the established business model of the music industry. This step explains what the emergence of Napster, the decline of CD sales, and the dramatic changes of the music industry have to do with the blockchain.

How a Peer-to-Peer System Changed a Whole Industry

The music industry has worked for a long time in the following way: musicians made contracts with studios, which recorded the songs, produced and marketed the music records on a variety of media (e.g., vinyl, tape, or CD), which in turn were sold to the customers via a variety of distribution channels, including department stores and specialized shops. The studios actually worked as intermediaries between musicians and people who enjoy listening to music. Music studios could maintain their role as intermediaries due to their exclusive knowledge and skills in producing, marketing, and distributing records. However, in the first decade of the 2000s, the environment in which the music studios operated changed dramatically.

The digitalization of music, the availability of recording equipment at affordable prices, the growing spread of privately used PCs, and the emergence of the Internet made music studios dispensable. The three functions of music studios—producing, marketing, and distributing records—could be done by the artists and the consumers themselves. Napster played a major role in the replacement of the music studios as intermediaries. With Napster, people no longer relied on the music studios to get the latest hits. It was possible to share individual music files with people all over the world without the need to buy any CDs. The peer-to-peer approach of Napster, actually being a kind of a digital sharing bazaar for mp3 files, gave consumers access to a wider range of music than ever before, making the music studios partly dispensable and causing them significant losses.[1]

The Potential of Peer-to-Peer Systems

The Napster case taught us that peer-to-peer systems have the potential to reshape whole industries based on a simple idea: replacing the middleman with peer-to-peer interactions. In the case of the music industry, the traditional studios and their marketing and distribution channels that acted as the middlemen between artists and consumers have been replaced by peer-to-peer file sharing systems. The major characteristics that made the music industry so vulnerable to being replaced by peer-to-peer systems are the immaterial nature of music and the low costs of copying and transferring data.

The power of peer-to-peer systems is not restricted to the music industry. Each industry that mainly acts as a middleman between producers and customers of immaterial or digital goods and services is vulnerable to being replaced by a peer-to-peer system. This statement may sound a bit abstract, but you may discover many middlemen for immaterial and digital goods and services around you once you recognize the largest of them all: the financial industry.

What is it that you have in your bank account or on your credit or debit card? Is it really money? The money you own has been turned into immaterial bits and bytes long ago. Only a small amount of actual money exists as physical banknotes and coins. The vast majority of the world's money and assets exists as immaterial bits and bytes in the centralized information technology systems of the financial industry. Banks and many other players of the financial industry are just middlemen between producers and consumers of bits and bytes that make up our money and our wealth. The act of borrowing, lending, or transferring money from one account to another is just the transfer of an immaterial good operated by middlemen, also called intermediaries. It is amazing how many middlemen are involved in seemingly simple transactions (e.g., transferring money from one bank account to another one in a different country involves up to five middlemen, which all need their processing time and impose their own fees). As a result, something as simple as transferring an amount of money from one bank account to another in a different country involves a long

---

[1]Hong, Seung-Hyun. The effect of Napster on recorded music sales: evidence from the consumer expenditure survey. *Stanford Institute for Economic Policy Research Working Paper* (2004): 3–18; Leyshon, Andrew. Scary monsters? Software formats, peer-to-peer networks, and the spectre of the gift. *Environment and Planning D: Society and Space* 21.5 (2003): 533–558.

processing time and incurs high transactions costs. In a peer-to-peer system, the same transfer would be much simpler and it would take less time and costs since it could be processed as what it is: a transfer of bits and bytes between two peers or nodes, respectively.

The advantage of peer-to-peer systems over centralized systems is that direct interactions occur between contractual partners instead of indirect interactions through a middleman, hence, there is less processing time and lower costs.

The advantages of peer-to-peer systems are not restricted to money transfer. Every industry that mainly acts as a middleman between producers and customers of immaterial or digital goods and services is vulnerable to being replaced by a peer-to-peer system. As digitalization continues, more and more items of everyday life and an increasing amount of goods and services will become immaterial and will benefit from the efficiencies of peer-to-peer systems. Advocates of peer-to-peer systems argue that almost all aspects of our life will be affected by the emergence of digitalization and peer-to-peer networks such as payments, money saving, loans, insurance, as well as issuance and validation of birth certificates, driving licenses, passports, identity cards, educational certificates, and patents and labor contracts. Most of them already exist in digital form in centralized systems run by institutions that are nothing other than a middleman between natural suppliers and customers.

■ **Note** Replacing the middleman is also called disintermediation. It is considered a serious threat to many business and companies that mainly act as intermediaries between different groups of people, such as buyers and seller, borrowers and lenders, or producers and consumers.

Terminology and the Link to the Blockchain

Now that you have learned about the potential of peer-to-peer systems, it is necessary to clarify the terminology of the problem domain and to explain its relation to the blockchain. In particular, the following points need to be discussed:

- The definition of a peer-to-peer system
- Architecture of peer-to-peer systems
- The link between peer-to-peer systems and the blockchain

The Definition of a Peer-to-Peer System

Peer-to-peer systems are distributed software systems that consist of nodes (individual computers), which make their computational resources (e.g., processing power, storage capacity, or information distribution) directly available to another. When joining a peer-to-peer system, users turn their computers into nodes of the system that are equal concerning their rights and roles. Although users may differ with respect to the resources they contribute, all the nodes in the system have the same functional capability and responsibility. Hence, the computers of all users are both suppliers and consumers of resources.[2]

For example, in a peer-to-peer file sharing system, the individual files are stored on the users' machines. When someone wants to download a file in such a system, he or she is downloading it from another person's machine, which could be the next door neighbor or someone located halfway around the world.

Architecture of Peer-to-Peer Systems

Peer-to-peer systems are distributed computer systems by construction since they are made of individual nodes that share their computational resources among others. However, there are also peer-to-peer systems that still utilize elements of centralization. Centralized peer-to-peer systems maintain central nodes to facilitate the interaction between peers, to maintain directories that describe the services offered by the peer nodes, or to perform look-ups and identification of the nodes.[3] Centralized peer-to-peer systems typically utilize a hybrid architecture, such as the one that was illustrated on the left-hand side of Figure 2-2. Such architecture allows combining the advantages of centralized and distributed computing. On the other hand, purely distributed peer-to-peer systems do not have any element of central control or coordination. Hence, all nodes in those systems perform the same tasks, acting both as providers and consumers of resources and services.

An example of a centralized peer-to-peer system is Napster, which maintained a central database of all nodes connected with the system and the songs available on these nodes.

---

[2]Tanenbaum, Andrew S., and Maarten Van Steen. *Distributed systems: principles and paradigms.* Upper Saddle River, NJ: Pearson Prentice Hall, 2007.

[3]Eberspächer, Jörg, and Rüdiger Schollmeier. First and second generation of peer-to-peer systems. In *Peer-to-peer systems and applications.* Berlin Heidelberg: Springer Verlag, 2005: 35–56.

The Link Between Peer-to-Peer Systems and the Blockchain

As discussed in Step 2, the blockchain can be considered a tool for achieving and maintaining integrity in distributed systems. Purely distributed peer-to-peer systems may use the blockchain in order to achieve and to maintain system integrity. Hence, the link between purely distributed peer-to-peer systems and the blockchain is its usage for achieving and maintaining integrity in purely distributed systems.

The Potential of the Blockchain

The relation between purely distributed peer-to-peer systems to the blockchain is that the former uses the latter as a tool to achieve and maintain integrity. Hence, the argument that explains the excitement about and the potential of the blockchain is: Purely distributed peer-to-peer systems have a huge commercial potential as they can replace centralized systems and change whole industries due to disintermediation. Since purely distributed peer-to-peer systems may use the blockchain for achieving and maintaining integrity, the blockchain becomes important as well. However, the major fact that excites people is the disintermediation. The blockchain is only a means to an end that helps to achieve that.

Note   The excitement about the blockchain is based on its ability to serve as a tool for achieving and maintaining integrity in purely distributed peer-to-peer systems that have the potential to change whole industries due to disintermediation.

Outlook

This step explained what peer-to-peer systems are and highlighted their potential to change whole industries due to disintermediation. Additionally, this step pointed out that the excitement about the blockchain is due to its ability to serve purely distributed peer-to-peer systems to fulfill their tasks. However, the question of why achieving and maintaining integrity in distributed systems is so important has not been answered yet. The next step will discuss that question in more detail.

Summary

- Peer-to-peer systems consist of computers, which make their computational resources directly available to another.

- The advantage of peer-to-peer systems is their ability to allow users to interact directly with one another instead of interacting indirectly through middlemen.

- Replacing middlemen with peer-to-peer systems increases processing speed and reduces costs.

- Peer-to-peer systems can be centralized or purely distributed.

- Purely distributed peer-to-peer systems form a network of equal members that interact directly with one another without having any central coordination.

- Napster demonstrated the power of peer-to-peer systems as its file sharing system ushered in a new era for the business model of the traditional music industry, which mainly acted as a middleman between artists and consumers.

- Every industry that mainly acts as a middleman between producers and customers of immaterial or digital goods and services is vulnerable to being replaced by peer-to-peer systems.

- A huge part of our financial system is simple intermediation between suppliers and consumers of money, which mainly exists as digital or immaterial good. Hence, digitalization and peer-to-peer systems may reshape the financial industry in a similar fashion as Napster reshaped the music industry.

- As digitalization continues, more aspects of our everyday lives and an increasing amount of goods and services will become immaterial and will benefit from the advantages of peer-to-peer systems.

- The excitement about the blockchain is based on its ability to serve as a tool for achieving and maintaining integrity in purely distributed peer-to-peer systems that have the potential to change whole industries due to disintermediation.

Why the Blockchain Is Needed

This stage explains the problem that the blockchain is supposed to solve and why solving this problem is important. This stage also deepens your understanding of the problem domain in which the blockchain is located, the environment in which it provides the most value, and its relation to trust, integrity, and the management of ownership. By the end of this stage, you will have gained a deeper understanding of the purpose of the blockchain and you will have reached a differentiated understanding of the term *blockchain* itself.

Discovering the Core Problem

How to herd a group of independent computers

The previous two steps pointed out the purpose of the blockchain in general and highlighted its importance for purely distributed peer-to-peer systems in particular. It turned out that maintaining integrity in distributed systems is the major purpose of the blockchain. But why is maintaining integrity in distributed systems and purely distributed peer-to-peer systems in particular such a challenge? This step answers that question by discovering the subtle relation between trust and integrity of purely distributed peer-to-peer systems. As a result, this step will deepen your understanding of the importance of integrity and uncovers the major problem to be solved by the blockchain. Finally, this step describes the environment in which the blockchain is expected to provide the most value.

The Metaphor

Many languages have a pictorial saying for describing the situation when someone tries to organize a chaotic group of individuals. For example, in English one would describe such a situation as trying to herd cats, as it illustrates the challenges of herding a group of obstinate and intractable animals that do not accept or even recognize a central authority. Does the problem of trying to organize a group of individuals who do not accept or recognize a

© Daniel Drescher 2017
D. Drescher, *Blockchain Basics*, DOI 10.1007/978-1-4842-2604-9_4

central authority sound familiar? It happens that this is exactly the situation of a purely distributed peer-to-peer system, which consists of individual and independent nodes without having any kind of central control or coordination. This step explains a major challenge of purely distributed peer-to-peer systems and how it relates to the blockchain.

Trust and Integrity in Peer-to-Peer Systems

Trust and integrity are two sides of the same coin. In the context of software systems, *integrity* is a nonfunctional aspect of a system to be safe, complete, consistent, correct, and free of corruption and errors. *Trust* is also the firm belief of humans in the reliability, truth, or ability of someone or something without evidence, proof, or investigation. Trust is given in advance and will increase or decline based on the results of interactions on an ongoing basis.

With respect to peer-to-peer systems, this means that people will join and continue to contribute to a system if they trust it and if the results of interacting with the system on an ongoing basis confirm and reinforce their trust. Integrity of the system is needed in order to fulfill the expectations of the users and reinforce their trust in the system. If the trust of the users is not reinforced by the system due to a lack of integrity, the users will abandon the system, which, as a result, will eventually cause it to terminate. Due to the importance of trust for the existence of peer-to-peer systems, the major question is: How do we achieve and maintain integrity in a purely distributed peer-to-peer system?

Achieving and maintaining integrity in purely distributed systems depends on a variety of factors, some of the most important are:

- Knowledge about the number of nodes or peers
- Knowledge about the trustworthiness of the peers

The chances of achieving integrity in a distributed peer-to-peer system are higher if the number of nodes as well as their trustworthiness is known. This situation is comparable to running a private club that adheres to high moral standards and utilizes a rigorous on-boarding process for new members. However, the worst circumstances for achieving integrity in a distributed peer-to-peer system are given when the number of nodes and their trustworthiness is unknown. This is the case when running a purely distributed peer-to-peer system on the Internet that is open to everyone.

Integrity Threats in Peer-to-Peer Systems

For simplicity, one can consider two major integrity threats in peer-to-peer systems:

- Technical failures
- Malicious peers

Technical Failures

Peer-to-peer systems are comprised of the individual computers of its users who communicate via a network. All hardware and software components of a computer system as well as any component of a computer network have the immanent risk of failing or creating errors. Hence, any distributed system has to face the problem that its components may fail or may produce wrong results by chance.

Malicious Peers

Malicious members are the second integrity threat in peer-to-peer systems. This source of untrustworthiness is not a technical problem, but rather a problem caused by the goals of the individuals who decide to exploit the system for their own purposes. One could say that this threat is more related to sociology and group dynamics than to technology. Dishonest and malicious peers comprise the most severe threat to the peer-to-peer system, because they attack the foundation on which any peer-to-peer system is built: trust. As soon as users can no longer trust their peers, they will turn away and stop contributing computational resources to the system. Hence, the number of members will decline and the whole system will become less attractive to the remaining members, which in turn will accelerate the decline of the system that eventually will be abandoned completely.

The Core Problem to Be Solved by the Blockchain

Achieving integrity and trust in the best of all conditions is easy. The real challenge is to achieve integrity and trust in a distributed system in the worst of all conditions. And this is the problem that the blockchain is supposed to solve. The core problem to be solved by the blockchain is achieving and maintaining integrity in a purely distributed peer-to-peer system that consists of an unknown number of peers with unknown reliability and trustworthiness. This problem is not a new one. It is actually a well-known and widely discussed problem in computer science. By utilizing a metaphor from the military, the problem is widely regarded as the Byzantine general problem.[1]

---

[1] Lamport, Leslie, Robert Shostak, and Marshall Pease. The Byzantine generals problem. *ACM Transactions on Programming Languages and Systems (TOPLAS)* 4.3 (1982): 382–401.

■ **Note**   The problem to be solved by the blockchain is achieving and maintaining integrity in a purely distributed peer-to-peer system that consists of an unknown number of peers with unknown reliability and trustworthiness.

Outlook

This step highlighted the importance of integrity and trust in peer-to-peer systems. Furthermore, this step pointed out the core problem to be solved by the blockchain and emphasized its importance for achieving integrity and trust in peer-to-peer systems. However, a definition of the term blockchain is still missing. This will be the subject of the next step.

Summary

- Integrity and trust are major concerns of peer-to-peer systems.

- People will join and continue to contribute to a peer-to-peer system if they trust it and if the results of interacting with the system on an ongoing basis confirm and reinforce that trust.

- As soon as people lose trust in a peer-to-peer system, they will abandon it, which in turn will cause the system to terminate eventually.

- Major integrity threats in peer-to-peer systems are:
  - Technical failures
  - Malicious peers

- Achieving integrity in a peer-to-peer system depends on:
  - The knowledge about the number of peers
  - The knowledge about the trustworthiness of the peers

- The core problem to be solved by the blockchain is achieving and maintaining integrity in a purely distributed peer-to-peer system that is comprised of an unknown number of peers with unknown reliability and trustworthiness.

Disambiguating the Term

Four ways to define the blockchain

In the preceding steps you learned about the major purpose of the block-chain and the relation between trust and integrity of the software system. As a result, you gained a well-grounded appreciation of the purpose of the blockchain, but you are still missing a definition of the term *blockchain* itself. This step will turn your attention to the definition of the term and explain its different usages. This step will present a provisional definition of blockchain, which will guide you through the remainder of this book. Finally, this step explains why the management of ownership is a prominent application case of the blockchain.

The Term

In this discussion about the blockchain, the term is used as follows:

- As a name for a data structure

- As a name for an algorithm

- As a name for a suite of technologies

- As an umbrella term for purely distributed peer-to-peer systems with a common application area

© Daniel Drescher 2017

D. Drescher, *Blockchain Basics*, DOI 10.1007/978-1-4842-2604-9_5

A Data Structure

In computer science and software engineering, a data structure is a way to organize data regardless of their concrete informational content. You can think about a data structure in terms of a floor plan for a building in architecture. A floor plan for a building addresses separating and connecting space with walls, floors, and stairs regardless of their concrete usage. When used as a name for a data structure, blockchain refers to data put together into units called blocks. One can think of these blocks much like pages in a book. These blocks are connected to one another like a chain, hence the name blockchain. In relation to a book, the words and sentences are the information to be stored. They are written on different pages instead of being written on a large spool. The pages are connected with one another via their position in the book and via the page numbers. You can determine if someone removed a page from the book by checking whether the page numbers continue without leaving out a number. Furthermore, the information on the pages as well as the pages within the book are ordered. The ordering is an important detail, which will be used extensively. Additionally, the chaining of the data blocks in the data structure is achieved by using a very special numbering system, which differs from the page numbering in ordinary books.

An Algorithm

In software engineering, the term *algorithm* refers to a sequence of instructions to be completed by a computer. These instructions often involve data structures. When used as a name for an algorithm, blockchain refers to a sequence of instructions that negotiates the informational content of many blockchain-data-structures in a purely distributed peer-to-peer system, similar to a democratic voting schema.

A Suite of Technologies

When used to refer to a suite of technologies, blockchain refers to a combination of the blockchain-data-structure, the blockchain-algorithm, as well as cryptographic and security technologies that combined can be used to achieve integrity in purely distributed peer-to-peer systems, regardless of the application goal.

An Umbrella Term for Purely Distributed Peer-to-Peer Systems with a Common Application Area

Blockchain can also be used as an umbrella term for purely distributed peer-to-peer systems of ledgers that utilize the blockchain-technology-suite. Note that in this context blockchain refers to a purely distributed system as a whole instead of referring to a software unit that is part of a purely distributed system.

The Usage of the Term in This Book

Throughout the rest of this book, blockchain refers to the shortcut for the umbrella term for purely distributed peer-to-peer systems of ledgers that utilize the blockchain-technology-suite. If any other meaning is intended, I will indicate this by explicitly using the term blockchain-data-structure, block-chain-algorithm, or blockchain-technology-suite.

■ **Note**   The technology that is nowadays regarded as blockchain was proposed in 2008 under the pseudonym Satoshi Nakamoto,[1] whose true identity has not yet been revealed.

Provisional Definition

The following definition is not complete. It still lacks important details that have not yet been presented. However, this definition serves as an intermediate step toward a more complete understanding of the term:

> *The blockchain is a purely distributed peer-to-peer system of ledgers that utilizes a software unit that consist of an algorithm, which negotiates the informational content of ordered and connected blocks of data together with cryptographic and security technologies in order to achieve and maintain its integrity.*

The Role of Managing Ownership

The provisional definition does not say anything about Bitcoin or managing ownership of cryptographic money. This may come as a surprise since many articles and books written about the blockchain claim that its purpose is to manage ownership of digital currencies. The truth is, managing ownership of cryptographic money is a very prominent and natural application case of the blockchain, but it is not the only one. The blockchain has a wide and diverse range of applications. However, there are two reasons why the management of ownership of digital goods is the most discussed application of the blockchain.

---

[1]Nakamoto, Satoshi. Bitcoin: a peer-to-peer electronic cash system. 2008. https://bitcoin.org/bitcoin.pdf.

First, it is the easiest to understand and to explain. Second, it is the use case with the most impact on the economy. The concept of ownership and the enforcement of ownership rights are core elements of almost every human society (even some animals have the concept of ownership and fight over its enforcement). A huge proportion of the activities of banks, insurance companies, custodians, lawyers, courts, solicitors, and consulates are concerned with just the management of ownership rights or their enforcement. Hence, managing ownership is a multibillion dollar market, and any technical innovation that could change the way we manage ownership will have a huge impact. It turns out that the blockchain can indeed dramatically change the way we manage ownership.

The Application Area of the Blockchain in This Book

The blockchain as a technology suite as used for managing distributed peer-to-peer systems of ledgers can have many specific applications such as managing ownership in digital goods or cryptographic currencies. However, this book deliberately does not consider just one specific application of the blockchain because I do not want to distract the attention from the core concepts by discussing just one specific application case in great detail. However, in order to make it easier for you to understand the blockchain, this book considers the general application case of managing and clarifying ownership regardless of the specific good whose ownership is managed. As a result, the general goal of managing and clarifying ownership will provide some mental guidance through your learning path and help to create a mental picture of the blockchain.

Outlook

This step clarified the term blockchain and provided a provisional definition. This book considers the general application case of managing and clarifying ownership in order to explain the blockchain, but there really needs to be a discussion of ownership in more detail. A more detailed understanding of ownership will help you to understand the functioning of the blockchain. The next step will explore the foundation of ownership in more detail.

Summary

- The term blockchain is ambiguous; it has different meanings for different people depending on the context.

- Blockchain can refer to:

  - A data structure

  - An algorithm

  - A suite of technologies

  - A group of purely distributed peer-to-peer systems with a common application area

- Managing and clarifying ownership is the most prominent application case of the blockchain but is not the only one.

- The blockchain is a purely distributed peer-to-peer system of ledgers that utilizes a software unit that consists of an algorithm, which negotiates the informational content of ordered and connected blocks of data together with cryptographic and security technologies in order to achieve and maintain its integrity.

Understanding the Nature of Ownership

Why we know what we own

Step 5 provided a preliminary definition of the blockchain and insight into why the management of ownership is regarded as its most prominent application case. This step deepens the relation between the blockchain and its prominent use case of managing ownership. In particular, this step reveals the connection between trust and integrity of purely distributed peer-to-peer systems, on the one hand, and managing ownership, on the other hand. In addition, this step also provides some general insights into the nature of ownership and introduces basic security concepts.

The Metaphor

Imagine the following situation. At home you are packing an apple into your bag for lunch. On your way to the office, you decide to go into a supermarket to buy a sandwich and some cookies. At the checkout point, you are opening your bag to collect the items you are buying. Just in this moment the employee

© Daniel Drescher 2017
D. Drescher, *Blockchain Basics*, DOI 10.1007/978-1-4842-2604-9_6

of the supermarket is looking at you and sees the apple in your bag, which happens to be the same kind of apples sold at the supermarket. What would the employee of the supermarket be thinking in this moment? He could falsely conclude from his observation that you may have stolen the apple from his store. Unfortunately, that supermarket does not have any supervision cameras or any security personnel, and you are the only customer at this moment. So how could you prove that you did not steal the apple?

Ownership and Witnesses

Have you ever thought about what makes you the owner of the things that belong to you? Probably, because you are still thinking about the apple in the supermarket story! So what makes you the owner of the apple in your bag? How can you prove that you have not stolen it from the supermarket?

So imagine you are in front of a court that disputes your alleged apple-theft case. How would you prove that you are the owner of the apple? We know that in the supermarket example, it would suffice to prove your innocence when no one could testify that you had stolen the apple. However, being discharged from the suspicion of being a thief is not proof of ownership. So let's stick to the question of proving your ownership.

It would be of great help if someone could testify that you had bought the apple *before* you went to the supermarket. Luckily, you remember the shop were you bought the apple and the employee who sold the apple to you is willing to testify to this. But you underestimated the prosecutor. He is talking to your witness in the cross-examination and asking your witness hard questions: Can he remember the apple he sold to you? Can he identify the specific apple he sold to you as the apple found in your bag? Can he identify you as the person who bought that particular apple? And finally why does he remember all these details in the first place? Could it be possible that you paid the witness money for testifying to your innocence? So this comes down to a basic principle: having one witness is good, but having many independent witnesses is the key to convincing the prosecutor of your innocence.

The last point is extremely important. The more independent witnesses who testify to the same fact, the higher the chance that this fact is indeed true. It turns out that this idea will be one of the core concepts of the blockchain.

Foundations of Ownership

Taking the findings of the previous section to a more abstract level, one can state that proving ownership involves three elements:

- An identification of the owner
- An identification of the object being owned
- A mapping of the owner to the object

The testimony of witnesses accomplishes all of these. Historically, eyewitnesses have often been the only source of clarifying these elements. However, relying on oral testimonies of witnesses is time-consuming. As a result, these elements have been replaced by documents issued by trustworthy entities. Nowadays, we can identify people with ID cards, birth certificates, and driver's licenses. Serial numbers, production dates, production certificates, or a detailed description can be used to identify objects. These documents do not change once they are created because the identities of people and objects do not change.

The mapping between owners and objects is typically done with a ledger or register. This is not a document that stays constant once created. Every transfer of ownership needs to be documented in such a register because an outdated register or ledger cannot be a trustworthy witness for testifying ownership. The importance of having an up-to-date and orderly managed register has led to the development of special institutions in many societies. The more valuable certain kinds of objects are, the higher the chance for the existence of a government-regulated ledger that documents the ownership of those objects. Most of these ledgers are open to everyone in order to make it easy to verify ownership and provide easy access to clarify ownership. You may do some research on your own to identify some of these ledgers in your country and to what they testify. I found ledgers for documenting ownership of real estate, patents, ships, airplanes, and companies. I even found registers for marriages, births, and deaths.

Figure 6-1 depicts the relation of the different concepts involved when designing software for managing ownership.

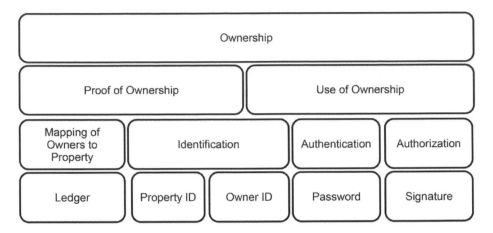

Figure 6-1. Concepts of ownership

In Figure 6-1, the concepts in the top layers are more general than those in the lower layers. The concepts on each layer can be seen as realizations of the concepts in layers above them. For example, the proof of ownership requires identification of owners and property alike as well as the mapping between owners and property. The use of ownership requires identification as well as authentication and authorization to ensure that only the legitimate person uses the property. The boxes in the very bottom row represent the implementation layer. They show, for example, that password and signature are concepts used to implement authentication and authorization. A ledger can be seen as a concrete implementation of a mapping between owners to their property.

A Short Detour to Security

Figure 6-1 used three major security related concepts that need to be explained in more detail, as their meaning in the context of software systems might be a bit different from their common usage:

- Identification

- Authentication

- Authorization

The meaning and interrelation of these three concepts can be illustrated by a real-world example. Perhaps you attempt to buy a bottle of wine in a liquor shop. Liquor shops are not allowed to sell alcoholic drinks to those who are underage. How does the liquor shop ensure that it sells wine only to the right people? The liquor shop accomplishes this by using identification, authentication, and authorization. And here is an explanation how this works.

Identification

Identification just means to claim to be someone by stating a name or anything else that could be used as an identifier.[1] In the liquor shop example, one could claim to be a certain person by stating a name. Identification does not prove that you really are who you claim to be. Identification does not involve the proof that you are not underage. Identification just means claiming to be a certain person.

Authentication

The purpose of authentication is to prevent someone from claiming to be someone else. Authentication means verifying or proving that you really are who you claim to be[1]. This proof can be provided by something you have or something you know that can serve as proof that you really are who you claim to be (e.g., an ID card, a driver's license, or some details of the life of the person you claim to be). It is important that the proof of your claimed identity is uniquely connected to you (e.g., a photograph of your face, a fingerprint, or something else that identifies you uniquely). In the liquor shop example, this means that you can prove that you really are who you claimed to be by showing a driver's license that contains a photograph of you. Comparing your face with the face shown on the photograph on the driver's license accomplishes the verification. If you look like the person in the photograph of the driver's license, the authentication is successful. Otherwise, the authentication fails. Double checking one's face with the photograph on the driver's license aims to prevent someone from using someone else's driver's license.

Authorization

Authorization means granting access to specific resources or services due to the characteristics or properties of one's identity[1]. Authorization is the consequence of both a successful authentication and evaluation of one's characteristics or rights. In the liquor shop example, authorization means to decide whether you are allowed to buy a bottle of wine based on the date of birth shown on your driver's license. The shop assistant will refuse to sell you a bottle of wine if you are too young based on the date of birth shown

[1]Van Tilborg, Henk, and Sushil Jajodia, eds. *Encyclopedia of cryptography and security*. New York: Springer Science & Business Media, 2014.

on your driver's license. Note that in this case the refusal is not due to a failed authentication. Identification and authentication worked well, and because of the correct identification, the shop assistant can identify you as an underage person. Hence, authorization is always the result of evaluating the characteristics or properties of the previously authenticated identity against some rules.

Note   Identification means claiming to be someone. Authentication means proving that you really are who you claimed to be. Authorization means getting access to something due to the previously authenticated identity.

Purposes and Properties of a Ledger

Figure 6-2 illustrates how the proof of ownership and transfer of ownership relate to the purpose and the properties of a ledger.

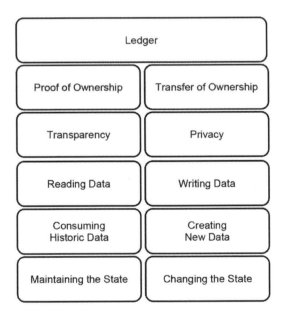

Figure 6-2. Concepts and principles of a ledger

The major lesson to be learned from Figure 6-2 is the fact that a ledger has to fulfill two opposing roles. On the one hand, a ledger serves as a means for proving ownership, which relies on reading historic data preserved in the ledger. On the other hand, the ledger has to document any transfer of ownership, which in turn implies that new data are produced and written to the ledger. One of the most important differences of these two purposes can be summarized in the opposing nature of transparency and privacy.

Proving ownership is easier when the ledger is open to anyone. Hence, transparency is the basis of proving ownership rights in a similar way as witnesses making a public testimony in court. However, transferring ownership must be exclusively restricted to the lawful owner. So privacy forms the basis of transferring ownership. Since writing in the ledger means changing ownership, only very trustful entities should be given writing access to ledgers.

The conflicting forces of transparency vs. privacy, proving ownership vs. transferring ownership, and reading the ledger vs. writing the ledger can also be found in the blockchain. It turns out that the blockchain is a gigantic distributed peer-to-peer system of ledger-like data structures that can be read by everyone.

Ownership and the Blockchain

A witness in the form of a government-regulated ledger is the key in clarifying ownership of valuable goods. But what happens if such a ledger is damaged or destroyed? Or what happens if someone responsible for updating the ledger makes an error or forges it on purpose? In this case, the ledger does not reflect reality. This is disastrous because everybody believes that the ledger represents the truth, similar to a witness in court.

The problem of having only one ledger as the source for clarifying ownership can be solved in the same way as it has been solved for trials in court. Basing a verdict only on the testimony of one single witness is risky since this witness could be dishonest. Having more witnesses is better. The more independent witnesses who are interrogated, the higher the chance that those facts that are consistently mentioned among the majority of testimonies reflect the truth. This fact can be proved by means of statistics and the law of large numbers. Having many witnesses who independently make their own observations free of mutual influences is the key for this approach to finding the truth.

Applying this finding to the use of a ledger for clarifying ownership is straightforward: Instead of maintaining only one single ledger that could be forged, one should utilize a purely distributed peer-to-peer system of ledgers and clarify requests concerning ownership on that version of the reality on which the majority of peers agrees.

At this point you might be wondering what all this has to do with the blockchain. The relation between managing ownership with a ledger and the blockchain is summed up as:

- An individual ledger is used for maintaining information about ownership, which is equivalent to one blockchain-data-structure storing ownership-related data.

- The individual ledgers are stored on the computers (nodes) of a peer-to-peer system.

- The blockchain-algorithm is responsible for letting the individual nodes collectively arrive at one consistent version of the state of ownership on which the final verdict is based.

- Integrity in this system is its ability to make true statements about ownership.

- Cryptography is necessary for creating a trustworthy means of identification, authentication, and authorization and ensuring data security.

Outlook

This step highlighted important characteristics of ownership and how they relate to the properties of ledgers. Furthermore, this step sketched how the blockchain relates to ownership and ledgers. The next step discusses an important consequence of having ownership managed in a purely distributed peer-to-peer system of ledgers.

Summary

- A proof of ownership has three elements:
  - Identification of the owner
  - Identification of the object being owned
  - Mapping the owner to the object
- ID cards, birth certificates, and driver's licenses as well as serial numbers, production dates, production certificates, or a detailed object description can be used in order to identify owners and objects.

- The mapping between owners and objects can be maintained in a ledger, which plays the same role as a witness in a trial.

- Having only one ledger is risky since it can be damaged, destroyed, or forged. In this case, the ledger is no longer a trustworthy source for clarifying ownership.

- Instead of using only one central ledger, one can utilize a group of independent ledgers for documenting ownership and clarify requests concerning the ownership on that version of the reality on which the majority of ledgers agrees.

- It is possible to create a purely distributed peer-to-peer system of ledgers by using the blockchain-data-structure. Each blockchain-data-structure represents one ledger and is maintained by one node of the system. The blockchain-algorithm is responsible for letting the individual nodes collectively arrive at one consistent version of the state of ownership. Cryptography is used to implement identification, authentication, and authorization.

- Integrity of a purely distributed peer-to-peer system of ledgers is found in its ability to make true statements about ownership and to ensure that only the lawful owner can transfer his or her property rights to others.

Spending Money Twice

Exploiting a vulnerability of distributed peer-to-peer systems

In the previous step, you learned about the relation between purely distributed peer-to-peer systems and the most prominent use case of the blockchain as a means to manage ownership. You also learned that the integrity of a distributed peer-to-peer system of ledgers is found in its ability to make true statements about ownership and to ensure that only the lawful owner can transfer his or her property rights to others. But what does this statement mean in real life? What happens if integrity is violated? This step considers these questions in more details. In particular, this step introduces one of the most important examples of violated integrity in distributed peer-to-peer systems: the double spending problem.

The Metaphor

Counterfeiting bank notes is a severe crime in any country because it undermines the foundation and functioning of the economy by creating purchasing power that is not backed up by valuable resources. As a result, most bank

© Daniel Drescher 2017

D. Drescher, *Blockchain Basics*, DOI 10.1007/978-1-4842-2604-9_7

notes are equipped with security features that make counterfeiting impossible or prohibitively costly at least. These security features, such as unique numbers, watermarks, or fluorescent fibers, work well with physical bank notes and other physical goods. But what happens if money or goods become digital and are managed in distributed peer-to-peer systems of ledgers? This step explains a specific vulnerability of distributed peer-to-peer systems used for managing ownership that is equivalent to counterfeiting bank notes. As it turns out, this vulnerability is a prominent example of violated system integrity.

The Double Spending Problem

Let's consider a peer-to-peer system for managing ownership of real estate. In such a system, the ledgers that keep track of ownership information are maintained by the individual computers of its members instead of being maintained in a central database. Hence, each peer maintains his or her own copy of the ledger. As soon as the ownership of a house is transferred from one person to another, all the ledgers of the system need to be updated in order to contain the latest version of reality. However, passing information forward among peers and updating the individual ledgers require time. Until the last member of the system receives the new information and updates his or her copy of the ledger, the system will not be consistent. Some peers already know about the latest transfer of ownership, while other peers have not yet received that information. The fact that not all ledgers have up-to-date information makes them prone to be exploited by anyone who already has the latest information.

Let's also imagine the following situation. Person A sells his house to person B. The transfer of ownership from A to B is documented in one of the ledgers in the peer-to-peer system. This particular ledger needs to inform other peers about this transfer, who in turn inform other peers as well, until eventually all peers learn about the transfer of ownership from A to B. However, suppose that person A quickly approaches another ledger of the system and demands to document a different transfer of ownership of the identical house: the sale from person A to person C. If this peer has not yet learned about the transfer of ownership from A to B that happened in the past, this peer will approve and document the transfer of ownership from A to C for the identical house. Hence, A was able to sell his house twice by exploiting the fact that distributing information about his first sell requires time. But B and C cannot own the house at the same time. Only one of them is supposed to be the new and lawful owner. Hence, the situation is called the double spending problem.

The Term

Similar to the term *blockchain*, the term *double spending* is ambiguous as it is used to refer to the following concepts:

- A problem caused by copying digital goods

- A problem that may appear in distributed peer-to-peer systems of ledgers

- An example of violated integrity in purely distributed peer-to-peer systems

Double Spending as a Problem of Copying Digital Goods

In the context of copying digital goods, the double spending problem refers to the fact that data on a computer can be copied without noticeable limitations. This fact causes problems with digital money or any other data that are supposed to have only one owner at a given time. Copying makes it possible to replicate data that represent pieces of digital money and use them more than once for making payments. This is the digital equivalent to replicating bank notes with a copying machine. Besides being technically possible, the copying of digital money violates the core principle of money: an identical piece of money cannot be given to different people at the same time. The ability to copy and spend digital money multiple times renders the money useless, hence, the double spending problem.

Double Spending as a Problem of Distributed Peer-to-Peer Systems of Ledgers

When used to describe the problem of a distributed peer-to-peer system of ledgers, double spending problem refers to the fact that forwarding information to all elements of such a system requires time, thus not all peers have the same ownership information at the same time. Because not all peers have up-to-date information, they are prone to be exploited by anyone who already has the latest information. As a result, one may be able to transfer ownership more than once, resulting in double spending.

Double Spending as an Example of Violated Integrity in Distributed Peer-to-Peer Systems

The use of distributed peer-to-peer systems is not restricted to managing ownership. However, the problem of forwarding information among peers and updating the data maintained by the members of the system stays the same, regardless of the specific application domain. Hence, on a more abstract level, the double spending problem can be seen as a problem of maintaining data consistency in distributed peer-to-peer systems. Since data consistency is one aspect of system integrity, one could say that the double spending problem is a specific example of violated system integrity.

How to Solve the Double Spending Problem

Because double spending can have different meanings, there is no single way to prevent it. Instead, many different solutions may exist. The following sections describe some of them.

Solving Double Spending as a Problem of Copying Digital Goods

The problem of spending digital money or any other digital assets more than once just by copying the data is actually a problem related to the nature of ownership. Any accepted means of mapping data that represents digital goods to their owners will solve that problem, regardless of its specific implementation. Even a physical central book or (more realistically) an electronic ledger, regardless of its architecture (centralized or peer-to-peer), can ensure that a digital good will only be spent once, provided the ledger works correctly all the time.

Solving Double Spending as a Problem of a Distributed Peer-to-Peer System of Ledgers

In this context, the architecture as well as the application domain of the system are given. Distributed peer-to-peer systems of ledgers are often regarded as the classical example to derive the blockchain. The explanations provided in Step 6 highlighted the relation between the blockchain and distributed peer-to-peer systems of ledgers. Hence, the blockchain, as this term is used throughout this book, can be seen as a solution to the double spending problem in a distributed peer-to-peer system of ledgers.

Solving Double Spending as an Example of Violated Integrity in Distributed Peer-to-Peer Systems

In this context, the architecture of the system is specified but the application domain is left unspecified. Hence, solutions on this level focus on achieving and maintaining integrity in distributed peer-to-peer systems, regardless of their concrete usage. However, the concrete usage of a distributed peer-to-peer system determines the meaning of integrity. For example, a simple file-sharing application may consider different aspects for defining integrity as compared to a system that manages ownership in a digital currency. Hence, the question of whether the blockchain-technology-suite is the right tool for achieving and maintaining system integrity cannot be answered without knowledge of the specific application goals. Hence, it could be possible that in specific application areas of distributed peer-to-peer systems, other technologies, data structures, and algorithms are more suitable for achieving and maintaining integrity.

Note The double spending problem is a prominent example of violated integrity in distributed peer-to-peer systems of ledgers, and the blockchain-technology-suite is a tool used to solve it.

The Usage of Double Spending in This Book

In this book the term *double spending* is used to refer to a vulnerability that may appear in purely distributed peer-to-peer systems of ledgers.

Outlook

This step explained double spending and highlighted the importance of the blockchain to achieve integrity in purely distributed peer-to-peer systems. The next steps focus on how the blockchain achieves and maintains integrity.

Summary

- The term *double spending* is ambiguous; it has different meanings.
- Double spending can refer to:
  - A problem caused by copying digital goods

- A problem that may appear in a distributed peer-to-peer system of ledgers

- An example of violating the integrity of distributed peer-to-peer systems

- In this book the term double spending is used to refer to a vulnerability of purely distributed peer-to-peer systems of ledgers.

- The blockchain is a means to solve the double spending problem.

How the Blockchain Works

This learning stage is the centerpiece of this book because it explains how the blockchain works internally. The 14 learning steps in this stage will guide you through all of the concepts of the blockchain and their underlying technologies. By the end of this stage, you will have reached a solid understanding of all the major concepts of the blockchain, how they work in isolation, and how they interact in order to create the big machinery that is called the blockchain.

Planning the Blockchain

The basic concepts of managing ownership with the blockchain

The preceding steps uncovered the relation between trust, integrity, purely distributed peer-to-peer systems, and the blockchain. As a result, you now have a good understanding of what the blockchain is, why it is needed, and what problem it solves. However, you still do not know how the blockchain works internally. This step provides a first impression of how the blockchain works by explaining the general application scenario that will guide you through the succeeding steps. It also highlights the major tasks in designing a blockchain for managing ownership and provides an overview of its major concepts. This step serves as the starting point for the succeeding steps that will discuss in great detail the concepts and technologies that make up the blockchain.

The Goal

The goal here is to understand the concepts that make up the blockchain. For didactical reasons, I will present the challenge of designing your own system for managing ownership. Hence, you will face the same challenges that

© Daniel Drescher 2017
D. Drescher, *Blockchain Basics*, DOI 10.1007/978-1-4842-2604-9_8

the inventor of the blockchain once faced and successfully solved: designing a piece of software that manages ownership in a purely distributed peer-to-peer system of ledgers that operates in a completely open and untrustworthy environment.

Starting Point

As a starting point, the major facts about the system under consideration can be summarized as following:

- The system will be a purely distributed peer-to-peer system, which is made of the computational resources contributed by its users.

- The peer-to-peer system uses the Internet as a network for connecting the individual nodes.

- Neither the number of nodes nor their trustworthiness and reliability is known.

- The goal of the peer-to-peer system is the management of ownership of a digital good (e.g., sales bonus points or digital money).

The Path to Follow

There are seven major tasks that need to be addressed when designing and developing a software system that manages ownership by using a purely distributed peer-to-peer system of ledgers in an open and untrustworthy environment:

- Describing ownership

- Protecting ownership

- Storing transaction data

- Preparing ledgers to be distributed in an untrustworthy environment

- Distributing the ledgers

- Adding new transaction to the ledgers

- Deciding which ledgers represents the truth

Task 1: Describing Ownership

Before you can start developing the blockchain, you need to ask yourself what you want to do with it. Since you will want to design a software system that manages ownership, you have to decide how to describe ownership first. It turns out that transactions are a good way to describe any transfer of ownership, and the complete history of transactions is the key to identifying the current owners. Hence, Step 9 will explain transactions, what they are, how you can describe them, and how you can use them to clarify ownership.

Task 2: Protecting Ownership

Describing ownership by using transactions is just the starting point. Moreover, you need a way to prevent people from accessing the property of others. In real life, you can easily prevent people from using your car or from entering your house by using doors with locks. It turns out that cryptography provides a way to protect transactions on an individual level, similar to the way doors with locks protect your individual car or house.

Protecting ownership has three major elements: identifying and authenticating owners as well as restricting access to the property to its owners. Steps 12 and 13 will explain these concepts in more details. However, these steps rely on the concept of hash values. If you have never heard about hash values before, you do not have to worry. I devoted Steps 10 and 11 to explaining hash values in great detail. These two steps will also offer interesting insights for those who already have a technical background or know about hash values.

Task 3: Storing Transaction Data

Describing ownership by means of transactions and having security measures that protect ownership on the level of individual transactions are important steps toward the goal of designing a software system that manages ownership. However, you need a way to store the whole history of transactions, as this history is used to clarify ownership. Since the transaction history is the core element in clarifying ownership, it must be stored in a secure way. It turns out that the blockchain-data-structure is the digital equivalent to a ledger. Steps 14 and 15 explain the requirement that the blockchain-data-structure has to fulfill in order to serve as a digital ledger and how it is implemented.

Task 4: Preparing Ledgers to Be Distributed in an Untrustworthy Environment

Having one isolated ledger or blockchain-data-structure that contains transaction data is great, but your aim is to design a distributed peer-to-peer system of ledgers that operates in an untrustworthy environment. Hence, you will have copies of the ledger running on untrustworthy nodes in an untrustworthy network. Furthermore, you will hand over the control of the ledgers to the whole network without having any central point of control or coordination. How can you prevent the ledgers from being forged or manipulated (e.g., by deleting transactions from the history or adding illegal transactions to it)? It turns out that the best way to prevent the transaction history from being changed is to make it unchangeable. This means the ledgers and therefore the transaction history cannot be changed once written. As a result, you will not have to fear that the ledgers will be tampered with or forged because they cannot be changed in the first place. However, having a distributed peer-to-peer system of ledgers that can never be changed sounds like a very secure but pretty useless thing because it will not allow you to add new transactions. Hence, the challenge of the blockchain-data-structure is to be unchangeable, on the one hand, while accepting new transactions being added to it, on the other hand. This sounds like a contradiction in terms, but it turns out that this is achievable with a technical trick that is explained in Step 16. The result is a blockchain-data-structure that is append-only: it is possible to add new transactions, but it is nearly impossible to change data that were added in the past.

Task 5: Distributing the Ledgers

Once the ledger is append-only, you can create a distributed peer-to-peer system of ledgers by making copies of it available to everyone who asks for it. However, just providing copies of append-only ledgers does not fulfill your goals. A distributed system that manages ownership involves interaction between the peers or nodes, respectively. Hence, Step 17 explains how the nodes in the system interact with one another and what information is exchanged among them.

Task 6: Adding New Transactions to the Ledgers

The distributed peer-to-peer system will consist of members whose computers maintain individual copies of an append-only blockchain-data-structure. Since the data structure allows you to add new transaction data, you will have to ensure that only valid and authorized transactions are added. It turns out that this is possible by allowing all members of the peer-to-peer system to add new data and additionally turning each member of the peer-to-peer system into supervisors of their peers. As a result, all members will supervise one another and point out any mistakes made by their peers. Step 18 explains this approach in more detail as well as the incentives given to the peers for fulfilling their role.

Task 7: Deciding Which Ledgers Represent the Truth

Once new transactions can be added to the individual ledgers in the peer-to-peer system, one runs into a problem that is typical for any distributed peer-to-peer system: different peers may have received different transactions and soon the history of transactions maintained by them differs. Hence, different versions of the transaction history can exist in the peer-to-peer system. Since the transaction history is the basis for identifying lawful owners, having different conflicting transaction histories is a serious threat to the integrity of the system. Hence, it is important to find a way either to prevent the emergence of different transaction histories in the first place or to find a way to decide which transaction history represents the truth. Due to the nature of a purely distributed peer-to-peer system, the former approach is not possible. As a result, you need a criterion for how to find and choose one transaction history that represents the truth. But there is another problem: there is no central authority in a purely distributed peer-to-peer system that can declare which transaction history has to be chosen. It turns out that one can solve that problem by making every node in the peer-to-peer system decide on its own which transaction history represents the truth in a way that the majority of the peers independently agree on that decision. It also turns out that the way in which the blockchain lets you add new transactions to the append-only blockchain-data-structure already contains the solution to this problem. Step 19 explains these criteria in detail and how they are used.

Outlook

This step identified seven tasks that provide a challenging intellectual journey through the concepts that constitute the blockchain. Once you fulfill these tasks, you will arrive at the summit: an understanding of the blockchain. Step 21 is the point where you will put all of these concepts together and enjoy the results of this learning effort. Step 21 will be an overview chapter like this one, but it will draw on the technical knowledge you will have acquired in the meantime.

Summary

- In order to design a purely distributed peer-to-peer system of ledgers for managing ownership, one has to address the following tasks:

  - Describing ownership

  - Protecting ownership from unauthorized access

  - Storing transaction data

  - Preparing ledgers to be distributed in an untrustworthy environment

  - Forming a system of distributed the ledgers

  - Adding and verifying new transactions to the ledgers

  - Deciding which ledgers represent the truth

- The tasks outlined above will be addressed in the following 12 steps.

Documenting Ownership

Using the course of history as evidence for the current state of ownership

This step considers the task of describing ownership in a way that is useful for a purely distributed peer-to-peer system of ledgers. This step explains how the blockchain documents ownership and handles the transfer of ownership. Additionally, this step points out the importance of ordering when documenting the transfer of ownership. Finally, this step highlights the importance of the integrity of transaction data for the integrity of the whole system.

The Metaphor

A relay race is a race between teams of runners, where each team member covers only a part of the total distance. During the race, each runner must hand off a specific item, the so-called baton, to the next runner within a certain zone marked on the track. At any given time during the race, only one member of the competing teams carries a baton. In order to determine which member of a given team is currently carrying the baton, it is sufficient to know to whom of the team the baton was handed over at the latest hand off.

© Daniel Drescher 2017
D. Drescher, *Blockchain Basics*, DOI 10.1007/978-1-4842-2604-9_9

In order to keep track of who carried a baton at any given time, one needs to record the time of each hand off and the athletes who were involved. This step explains how the blockchain treats ownership in a similar fashion to that of the way relay races utilize batons.

The Goal

The goal is the documentation of ownership in a transparent and comprehensible way. Anyone who reads that documentation should be able to make an unambiguous statement concerning the association of the goods to its owners.

The Challenge

The challenge is to find documentation of ownership that not just claims that someone is the owner of something, but also provides evidence of ownership and hence serves as proof of ownership.

The Idea

Instead of describing the current state of ownership by inventory data (i.e., by listing the current possessions of all owners), one maintains a list of all transfers of ownership in a ledger in an ongoing fashion. Every transfer of ownership is described by transaction data that clearly point out which owner hands off ownership of what item and to whom at what time. The whole history of transaction data stored in a ledger becomes an audit trail that provides evidence of how everyone achieved his or her possession.[1] This is equivalent to tracking every hand off of the baton in a relay race, which allows everyone to reconstruct the whole race later on.

A Short Detour to Inventory and Transaction Data

There are two competing ways to describe ownership—through inventory data or transaction data. *Inventory data* describe the current state of ownership. They are similar to a bank account statement that just displays the amount of money that is currently available. *Transaction data* describe transfers of ownership. They are similar to a bank account statement that lists every

---

[1]Nakamoto, Satoshi. Bitcoin: A peer-to-peer electronic cash system (2008).

withdrawal, deposit, and transferal of money. One can derive inventory data by aggregating transaction data. Besides the fact that both inventory data and transaction data describe ownership, their underlying philosophy differs dramatically. Inventory data just state or claim ownership, while transaction data explain and thereby justify ownership. However, inventory data are often considered more convenient as they immediately state the fact that is interesting to most people, that is, the current state of ownership.

How It Works

Documenting ownership with the blockchain involves the following aspects:

- Describing the transfer of ownership
- Maintaining the history of transfers

Describing the Transfer of Ownership

A *transaction* is the act of transferring ownership from one owner to someone else. The act of transferring ownership relies on data that descibe the intended transfer. These data contain all information necessary to execute the transfer of ownership. An example of data that describe an intended transfer of ownership would be a bank transfer form that is used to request a bank to make a money transfer on behalf of a customer. The bank transfer form requires you to provide all information necessary to allow the bank to make the transfer on your behalf. In a similar fashion, the information used by the blockchain to describe a transaction are:

- An identifier of the account that is to hand off ownership to another account
- An identifier of the account that is to receive ownership
- The amount of the goods to be transferred
- The time the transaction is to be done
- A fee to be paid to the system for executing the transaction
- A proof that the owner of the account that hands off ownership indeed agrees with that transfer

Most of these data are familiar to anyone who has made a money transfer with a bank. However, the analogy with a bank transfer ends when fees are considered. Due to the fact that banks are centralized institutions, they maintain a central fee schedule that is applied to all customers. In contrast to that, the blockchain is a distributed system without any central point of control. Hence, the blockchain cannot have a central fee schedule. When using the blockchain, each user has to tell the system in advance how much he or she is willing to pay for having the transaction executed. The account that hands off ownership also pays the transaction fee.

Maintaining the History of Transfers

Transaction data provide the mandatory information necessary to execute a transfer of ownership as intended. Executing a transaction means making the transfer of ownership happen as described by the transaction data. Executing a transaction means adding the transaction data to a ledger. By adding transaction data to a ledger, the transaction becomes part of the transaction history, which is used to clarify ownership. When the ledger is used the next time to clarify ownership by aggregating the transaction data it contains, the newly added transaction will be included in the aggregation and hence will impact the resulting state of ownership.

The blockchain maintains the whole history of all transactions that have ever happened by storing their transaction data in the blockchain-data-structure in the order in which they occurred. Any transaction not being part of that history is regarded as if it never happened. Hence, adding transaction data to the blockchain-data-structure means making this transaction happen and allowing it to influence the result of using the history in order to identify the current owner.

Why It Works

Since transaction data contain all the information about the account that hands off ownership, the account that receives ownership, and the item and the amount to be transferred, one can reconstruct ownership information for each account as long as the whole history of transactions is available. As a result, the whole history of all transaction data is sufficient to document ownership.

Importance of Ordering

Aggregating transaction data is done for the purpose of recovering the current state of ownership and clarifying ownership. It is important to recognize that the order in which the transactions occurred must be preserved in order to arrive at the identical result every time the data are aggregated. Changing the order of transaction data will change the result of aggregating them. At first glance, the result does not seem to change very much whether I receive a payment of $50 from a friend first and transferred $50 afterward in order to pay a bill or whether these two transactions occurred in the opposite order. But what happens if my bank account does not contain any money at all and I am not allowed to overdraw it? In this case, my ability to pay my bill depends on having received the payment from my friend first. Otherwise, the bank will refuse to transfer the money to pay the bill due to a lack of funds. Hence, the order in which transactions occur does indeed matter.

Integrity of the Transaction History

Without exaggeration, one can state that the history of transaction data is the heart of any blockchain that manages ownership because it is the basis for reconstructing the state of ownership. As a result, it is necessary to keep that history of data safe, complete, correct, and consistent in order to maintain the integrity of the whole system and, as a result, be able to make true statements regarding the current state of ownership. Hence, the blockchain needs to provide security measures to ensure that only valid transaction data are added to the blockchain-data-structure. Examining validity of transaction data involves three aspects:

- Formal correctness
- Semantic correctness
- Authorization

Formal Correctness

Formal correctness means that the description of a transaction contains all required data and that the data are provided in the correct format.

Semantic Correctness

Semantic correctness focuses on the meaning of transaction data and their intended effect. Hence, validating semantic correctness requires knowledge of the business domain. Examining semantic correctness of transaction data is often done based on business rules, such as:

- Ensuring that an account does not hand off more than it currently owns
- Preventing double spending
- Limiting the amount of items that can be transferred in a single transaction
- Limiting the number of transactions per user
- Limiting the total amount of items spent in a given time period
- Enforcing that an account keeps an item for a minimum time period before it can be transferred further

Authorization

Only the owner of the account who hands off ownership should be allowed to advise the blockchain to execute a transaction on his or her behalf. As a result, the blockchain requires every transaction to carry information that proves that the owner of the account who hands off ownership indeed agrees with that transfer.

Outlook

This step explained transactions and their role for clarifying ownership. The following steps are mainly concerned with how the blockchain enforces that only valid transaction data are added to the history and how the history is protected from being manipulated or forged.

Summary

- Transaction data provide the following information for describing a transfer of ownership:

    - An identifier of the account who initiates the transaction and is to transfer ownership to another account

    - An identifier of that account that is to receive ownership

    - The amount of the goods to be transferred

    - The time the transaction is to be done

    - A fee to be paid to the system for executing the transaction

    - A proof that the owner of the account who hands off ownership agrees with that transfer

- The complete history of transaction data is an audit trail that provides evidence of how people acquired and handed off ownership.

- Any transaction not being part of that history is regarded as if it never happened.

- A transaction is executed by adding it to the history of transaction data and allowing it to influence the result of aggregating them.

- The order in which transaction data are added to the history must be preserved in order to yield identical results when aggregating these data.

- In order to maintain integrity, only those transaction data are added to the blockchain-data-structure that fulfill the following three criteria:

  - Formal correctness

  - Semantic correctness

  - Authorization

Hashing Data

Identifying data from their digital fingerprint

This step explains one of the most important base technologies of the blockchain: hash values. It discusses important properties of cryptographic hash functions and introduces patterns of applying hash functions to data.

The Metaphor

Fingerprints are impressions of the friction ridges of all or any part of the fingers of the human hand. They are considered to be able to identify humans uniquely. They have been used to investigate crimes, identify offenders, and to exonerate the innocent. This step introduces a concept for identifying data, which can be seen as the digital equivalent to fingerprints. The concept is called cryptographic hash value, and the blockchain makes extensive use of it. Hence, understanding cryptographic hashing is mandatory for understanding the blockchain.

The Goal

In the distributed peer-to-peer system, you will deal with a huge number of transaction data. As a result, you will need to identify them uniquely and compare them as quickly and as easily as possible. Hence, the goal is to identify transaction data and possibly any kind of data uniquely by their digital fingerprints.

© Daniel Drescher 2017
D. Drescher, *Blockchain Basics*, DOI 10.1007/978-1-4842-2604-9_10

How It Works

Hash functions are small computer programs that transform any kind of data into a number of fixed lengths, regardless of the size of the input data.[1] Hash functions only accept one piece of data at any given time as input and create a hash value based on the bits and bytes that make up the data. Hash values can have leading zeros in order to provide the required length. There are many different hash functions that differ among others with respect to the length of the hash value they produce. An important group of hash functions is called *cryptographic hash functions*, which create digital fingerprints for any kind of data. Cryptographic hash functions have the following properties[2]:

- Providing hash values for any kind of data quickly

- Being deterministic

- Being pseudorandom

- Being one-way functions

- Being collision resistant

Providing Hash Values for Any Data Quickly

This property is actually a combination of two properties. First, the hash function is able to calculate hash values for all kinds of data. Second, the hash function does its calculation quickly. These properties are important, as you do not want the hash function to yield useless things like error messages or to take a large amount of time to return the results.

Deterministic

Deterministic means that the hash function yields identical hash values for identical input data. This means that any observed discrepancies of the hash values of data must be solely caused by the discrepancies of the input data and not by the internals of the hash function.

---

[1] Weisstein, Eric W. Hash function. From MathWorld: http://mathworld.wolfram.com/HashFunction.html.

[2] Rogaway, Phillip, and Thomas Shrimpton. Cryptographic hash-function basics: definitions, implications, and separations for preimage resistance, second-preimage resistance, and collision resistance. In B. Roy and W. Meier (eds.), *Fast software encryption. FSE 2004. Lecture Notes in Computer Science,* vol. 3017. International Workshop on Fast Software Encryption. Berlin Heidelberg: Springer, 2004.

Pseudorandom

Being pseudorandom means that the hash value returned by a hash function changes unpredictably when the input data are changed. Even if the input data were changed only a little bit, the resulting hash value will differ unpredictably. To put it differently, the hash value of changed data must always be a surprise. It should not be possible to predict the hash value based on the input data.

One-Way Function

A one-way function does not provide any way to trace its input values by its outputs. Hence, being a one-way function means that it cannot be used the other way around. To put it differently, it is impossible to recover the original input data based on the hash value. This means that hash values do not tell you anything about the content of the input data in the same way as an isolated fingerprint does not tell you anything about the person whose finger created it. One-way functions are also said to be noninvertible.

Collision Resistant

A hash function is called collision resistant if it is very hard to find two or more distinct pieces of data for which it yields the identical hash value. Or, to put it differently, if the chance to receive an identical hash value for distinct pieces of data is small, then the hash function is collision resistant. In this case, you can consider the hash values created by the hash function as being unique and hence being usable to identify data. If you obtained an identical hash value for different pieces of data, you would face a hash collision. A hash collision is the digital equivalent to having two people with identical fingerprints. Being collision resistant is mandatory for hash values to be usable as digital fingerprints. How collision resistant hash functions work internally is beyond the scope of this book, but you can be assured that huge effort has been spent on reducing their risk to produce hash collisions.

Trying It Out Yourself

This section will help you become comfortable with applying hash functions by guiding you through a simple example. For this purpose, I refer to the accompanying website that provides a tool for creating hash values of simple text data: http://www.blockchain-basics.com/HashFunctions.html.

When you open that webpage in your Internet browser, you will see an input box and an output box, as shown in Figure 10-1. Type the text Hello World! in the input box on the left-hand side and click the button with the label "Calculate Hash Value" located below the text field. Make sure that you type Hello World! exactly in the input box, otherwise you will get results that differ from those shown in Figure 10-1.

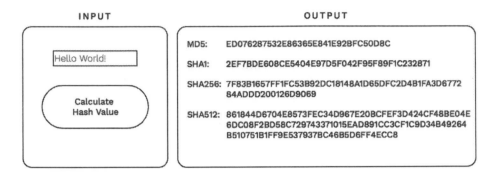

INPUT

OUTPUT

Hello World!

Calculate
Hash Value

MD5:   ED076287532E86365E841E92BFC50D8C

SHA1:   2EF7BDE608CE5404E97D5F042F95F89F1C232871

SHA256: 7F83B1657FF1FC53B92DC18148A1D65DFC2D4B1FA3D6772
        84ADDD200126D9069

SHA512: 861844D6704E8573FEC34D967E20BCFEF3D424CF48BE04E
        6DC08F2BD58C729743371015EAD891CC3CF1C9D34B49264
        B510751B1FF9E537937BC46B5D6FF4ECC8

Figure 10-1. Calculating hash values of a short text

As a result of clicking the button, the output box on the right-hand side will present the hash value of the input text calculated with four different hash functions. Hash values are often regarded as hash numbers since they use not only the digits 0 to 9 but also the letters A to F, which represent the values 11 to 16 in order to express numerical values. Those numbers are called *hexadecimal numbers*. Computer scientists love them for reasons I do not want discuss here. Notice that the hash values differ due to the different implementation details of the hash functions that produce them. These values are taken for granted, since we do not want to lose ourselves in the wide topic of implementation of hash functions.

Cryptographic hash values are quite long and therefore hard to read or to compare for the human eye. However, in the course of this step, you will compare different ways of hashing data, which involves reading and comparing hash values. Doing so with cryptographic hash values will quickly become a tedious task. Hence, for didactical reasons, I use a shortened version of the SHA256 cryptographic hash value in the remainder of this step. You can reproduce all hash values by using the tool provided on the accompanying website: www.blockchain-basics.com/Hashing.html.

When you open that website in your Internet browser, you will see an input box for simple texts, a button with an arrow that points to an output box, as shown in Figure 10-2. When you click the button with the arrow, the output box will present the shortened hash value of the text provided in the input box.

INPUT   CALCULATE   OUTPUT
              HASH VALUE

Hello World!   7F83B165

Figure 10-2. Calculating the shortened hash value of a text

Patterns of Hashing Data

So far you have learned that a piece of data can be used as input for a hash function, which in turn yields the hash value of that data. This implies that each independent piece of data has its own unique cryptographic hash value. But what would you do if you were asked to provide one single hash value for a bunch of independent pieces of data? Remember, hash functions only accept one piece of data at a given time. There is no hash function that accepts a bunch of independent data at once, but, in reality, we often need one single hash value for a large collection of data. In particular, the blockchain-data-structure has to deal with many transaction data at once and requires one single hash value for all of them. How do you deal with this task?

The answer is to utilize one of the following patterns in applying hash functions to data:

- Independent hashing
- Repeated hashing
- Combined hashing
- Sequential hashing
- Hierarchical hashing

Independent Hashing

Independent hashing means applying the hash function to each piece of data independently. Figure 10-3 illustrates this concept by calculating the shortened hash value of two distinct words separately.

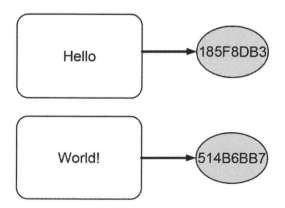

Figure 10-3. Schematic illustration of hashing different data independently

The white boxes that each contain a word represent the data to be hashed and the gray circles exhibit the corresponding hash values. The arrows that point from the boxes to the circles schematically illustrate the transformation of data into hash values. As one can see in Figure 10-3, the distinct words yield different hash values.

Repeated Hashing

You have learned that hash functions transform any arbitrary piece of data into a hash value. A hash value itself can be considered a piece of data. Hence, it should be possible to provide a hash value as input to a hash function and calculate its hash value too. And this in fact works! Repeated hashing is the repeated application of a hash function to its own outcome. Figure 10-4 illustrates the concept by calculating the shortened hash value repeatedly. The text Hello World! yields the hash value 7F83B165, which in turn yields the shortened hash value of 45A47BE7.

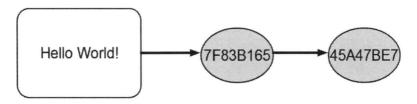

Figure 10-4. Calculating hash values repeatedly

Combined Hashing

The goal of combined hashing is to get a single hash value for more than one piece of data in one attempt. Combining all independent pieces of data into one piece of data and calculating its hash value afterward is the way to achieve this. This is in particular useful if you want to create one single hash value for a collection of data that is available at a given time. Since combining data costs computing power, time, and memory space, combined hashing should only be used when the individual pieces of data are small. Another drawback of combined hashing is that the hash values of the individual pieces of data are not available since only the combined data are handed over to the hash function.

Figure 10-5 depicts the concept of combined hashing. The individual words are first combined into one word with a letter space between them and the resulting phrase is hashed afterward. The resulting hash value shown in Figure 10-5 is consequently identical to the first hash value in Figure 10-4. Note that the hash value of the combined data critically depends on the way the data are combined. In Figure 10-4, the two words were combined by writing them next to each other with a letter space between them, which consequently yields Hello World! Sometimes specific symbols such as the plus sign (+) or hashtag sign (#) are used to mark the point where the data are connected, which, as a result, influences the resulting hash value.

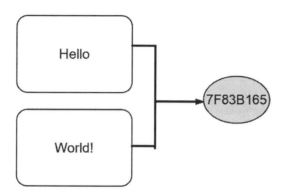

Figure 10-5. Combining data and subsequently calculating the hash value

Sequential Hashing

The goal of sequential hashing is the incremental update of a hash value as new data arrive. This is achieved by using combined and repeated hashing at the same time. The existing hash value is combined with new data and is then handed over to the hash function in order to get the updated hash value. Sequential hashing is in particular useful if you want to maintain a single hash value over time and update it as soon as new data arrive. An advantage of this type of hashing is that at any given point in time you have a hash value whose evolution can be traced back to the arrival of new data.

Figure 10-6 illustrates the concept of sequential hashing by starting with hashing the word Hello individually, which yields the shortened hash value 185F8DB3. Once new data represented by the word World! arrive, it is combined with the existing hash value and provided as input to a hash function. The hash value 5795A986 is the shortened hash value of the input text World! 185F8DB3.

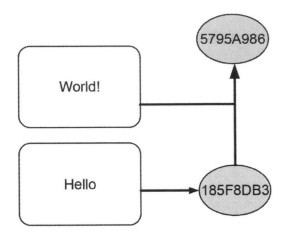

Figure 10-6. Calculating hash values sequentially

Hierarchical Hashing

Figure 10-7 illustrates the concept of hierarchical hashing.

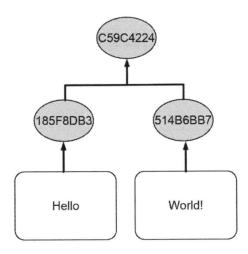

Figure 10-7. Calculating hash values hierarchically

The application of combined hashing to a pair of hash values forms a small hierarchy of hash values with a single value on its top. Similar to combined hashing, the idea of hierarchical hashing is the creation of one single hash value for a collection of data. Hierarchical hashing is more efficient because it combines hash values that are always of fixed size instead of the original data that could be of any size. Additionally, hierarchical hashing only combines two hash values in every step, while combined hashing will combine as many data as you provide in one attempt.

Outlook

This step was devoted to the concept of hash functions. Step 11 illustrates how hash values are used in real life and highlights how the blockchain uses them.

Summary

- Hash functions transform any kind of data into a number of fixed length, regardless of the size of the input data.

- There are many different hash functions that differ among others with respect to the length of the hash value they produce.

- Cryptographic hash functions are an important group of hash functions that create digital fingerprints for any kind of data.

- Cryptographic hash functions exhibit the following properties:
  - Provide hash values for any kind of data quickly
  - Deterministic
  - Pseudorandom
  - One-way usage
  - Collision resistant

- Application of hash functions to data can be accomplished by using the following patterns:
  - Repeated hashing
  - Independent hashing
  - Combined hashing
  - Sequential hashing
  - Hierarchical hashing

Hashing in the Real World

A tale of comparing data and creating computational puzzles

Step 10 introduced cryptographic hash functions and discussed different patterns of applying hash functions to data. Step 10 may have appeared to be a dry intellectual exercise, but it is actually of highly practical relevance. Hence, this step focuses on the application of hash functions and hash values in the real world. It considers major use cases of hash functions in real life and explains the idea behind them. This step also sketches why these use cases work out as intended. Finally, this step points out where the blockchain uses hash values.

Comparing Data

Because it is the most straightforward use case of hash values, comparing data based on their hash values is considered first.

The Goal

The goal is to compare data (e.g., files or transaction data) without comparing their content piece by piece and to make comparing any kind of data, regardless of their size and content, as easy as comparing two numbers.

© Daniel Drescher 2017
D. Drescher, *Blockchain Basics*, DOI 10.1007/978-1-4842-2604-9_11

The Idea

Instead of comparing data by explicitly comparing their content piece by piece, you compare their cryptographic hash values.

How It Works

You calculate and compare the cryptographic hash value of all data under consideration. If all of the cryptographic hash values differ, all the data under consideration differ as well. If two or more of the cryptographic hash values are identical, their corresponding input data are also identical.[1]

Why It Works

Comparing data by comparing their cryptographic hash values works due to collision resistance of cryptographic hash functions.

Detecting Changes in Data

The idea of comparing data based on their hash values can be easily extended to the case of detecting changes.

The Goal

The goal is to determine whether data (e.g., a file or transaction data) that is supposed to stay unchanged was changed after a certain date or after sending it to someone or after it was stored in a database.

The Idea

Comparing the cryptographic hash value of the data under consideration that was created in the past with a newly created cryptographic hash value of the same data is the key in identifying changes. If both hash values are identical, the data were not changed after the time at which the old hash value was created.

How It Works

You create the cryptographic hash value of the data that are supposed to stay unchanged. When you need to verify whether the data were changed at a later time, you create the cryptographic hash value of the data again. You then compare the newly created hash value with the hash value that was created

---

[1]Tsudik, Gene. Message authentication with one-way hash functions. *ACM SIGCOMM Computer Communication Review* 22.5 (1992): 29–38.

in the past. If both hash values are identical, the data were not changed after the first hash value was created. Otherwise, the data have been changed in the meantime. The same idea can be applied when sending data to someone. If you create the hash value of the data before they are sent and the receiver creates the hash value of the data he or she receives, both the sender and the receiver compare both hash values. If both hash values are identical, the data were not altered in the course of the transfer.

Why It Works

Detecting changes in data is actually a process of comparing data with themselves before and after certain events, such as lapses of time, storing to or retrieval from a database, or sending them through a network. Detecting changes in data that are supposed to stay unchanged works due to collision resistance of cryptographic hash functions.

Referring to Data in a Change-Sensitive Manner

Comparing data and detecting changes based on their hash values can be considered basic use cases of hash values. A slightly more advanced application case of hash values is hash references, which are introduced in the following.

The Goal

The goal is to refer to data (e.g., transaction data) that are stored somewhere else (e.g., on a hard disk or in a database) and ensure that the data have remain unchanged.

The Idea

The idea is to combine the cryptographic hash value of the data being stored with information about the place where the data are located. If the data were changed, both pieces of information would no longer be consistent and hence the hash reference would become invalid.

How It Works

References to data are the digital equivalent to cloakroom tickets. Cloakroom tickets point to the physical location at which your jacket is stored in the cloakroom. You use the cloakroom ticket for retrieving your jacket later on. References to data in computers work the same way: they are pieces of data that refer to other data. Computer programs use references in order to remember the place where the data have been stored and to retrieve them later on. Hash references are a specific kind of reference that utilize the power of cryptographic hash values. For simplicity, you could think of hash references as cloakroom tickets that display hash values instead of ordinary numbers.

Hash references refer to other data, and they additionally verify that the data being referred to were not changed since the reference was created. In the case where the data being referred have been changed, the reference no longer allows retrieval of the data. In this case, the hash reference is deemed broken or invalid. This is similar to having a cloakroom ticket that points to a coat hook that no longer carries your jacket. In this case, the cloakroom attendant can no longer hand over your jacket.

The whole idea of hash reference is to protect its users from retrieving data that have been changed accidently due to technical errors or intentionally by someone else without informing you about that. Hence, hash references are used in all occasions where data are supposed to stay unchanged once created.

A Schematic Illustration

The blockchain heavily depends on hash references. Hence, understanding them is crucial for understanding the blockchain and for comprehending the following steps of this book. For this reason, the following three figures serve two purposes: First, they schematically illustrate the functioning of hash references. Second, they introduce a pictorial representation of hash references that is used in the following steps when illustrating the functioning of the blockchain-data-structure.

Figure 11-1 illustrates the functioning of hash references schematically by presenting a valid hash reference. The gray circle labeled R1 represents a valid hash reference. The white box represents some data that are supposed to stay unchanged. The arrow that goes from the circle to the box depicts the functioning of the hash reference. The arrow points from the reference to the data it refers to.

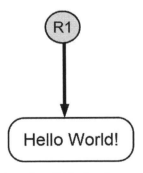

Figure 11-1. Schematic illustration of a valid hash reference

Figure 11-2 illustrates the symbolic representation of a broken or invalid hash reference.

Figure 11-2. Schematic illustration of an invalid hash reference

The black box containing a modified greeting represents data that were altered after the reference was created. The gray circle still represents the originally created hash reference. The jacked arrow that points from the circle to the altered box highlights that the hash reference R1 is broken, it no longer allows access to retrieve the data because they have been changed in the meantime.

Figure 11-3 illustrates the situation when a new hash reference was created after the data were changed. This situation is depicted by a black box representing altered data, a black circle representing a newly created hash reference, and the straight arrow pointing from the circle to the box.

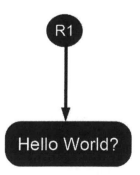

Figure 11-3. Schematic illustration of a newly created hash reference after altering the data being referred

Why It Works

The key point of hash references is the fact that they utilize cryptographic hash values, which can be seen as unique fingerprints of data. Hence, it is very unlikely to have two different pieces of data that have an identical hash value. As a result, a broken hash reference is considered to be evidence that the data were altered after the hash reference was created.

Storing Data in a Change-Sensitive Manner

The idea of referring to data based on their hash values can be extended further. A natural extension of that idea is storing data in a change-sensitive manner.

The Goal

The goal is to store a large amount of data e.g., transaction data that are supposed to stay unchanged. Any changes to these data are to be detected quickly and easily.

The Idea

Cloakroom tickets point to coat hooks that carry jackets. This is simple and straightforward. But what precludes you from putting a cloakroom ticket in the pocket of another jacket and storing that second jacket in the cloakroom as well? As a result, the latter cloakroom ticket points to a jacket that contains a cloakroom ticket, which in turn points to another jacket. Actually you can create long and complicated chains of jackets that have cloakroom tickets in their pockets, which point to other jackets, which also have a cloakroom ticket in their pockets, and so on and so forth. In a similar fashion, one can store data together with hash references that point to other data, which in turn store hash reference that refer to further data, and so on and so forth. If any of the data or hash references is changed after their creation, all the hash references are broken. Since broken hash references serve as evidence that data were changed after the reference was created, the whole construct stores data in a change-sensitive manner.

How It Works

There are two classical patterns of using hash references in order to store data in a change-sensitive manner:

- The chain
- The tree

The Chain

A chain of linked data, also called a linked list,[2] is formed when each piece of data also contains a hash reference to another piece of data. Such a structure is useful for storing and linking data together that are not fully available at one given point in time but instead arrive step by step in an ongoing fashion. Figure 11-4 illustrates this idea by using the symbols introduced above. The creation of such a chain starts with the piece of data labeled Data 1 and the creation of the hash reference R1. Being the first piece of data, Data 1 does not contain any hash reference. When new data arrive, they are put together with the hash reference that points to Data 1. The hash reference R2 refers to the newly arrived data and the hash reference R1. The hash reference R3, which refers to Data 3 and the hash reference R2, is created in a similar fashion.

Figure 11-4. Data linked together in a chain-like fashion

Hash reference R3 is all you need in order to access all the data in the chain in the reverse order of their arrival. The reference R3 is also called the **head of the chain** because it refers to the most currently added piece of data. It is important not to mix up the term "**head**" (that is the most currently added piece of data) with the term "**header**", which will be introduced in Step 14 when we discuss the blockchain-data-structure.

The Tree

Figure 11-5 illustrates how transaction data can be linked together with hash references in a tree-like fashion.

---

[2]Cormen, Thomas H. *Introduction to algorithms* (3rd ed.). Cambridge: MIT Press, 2009.

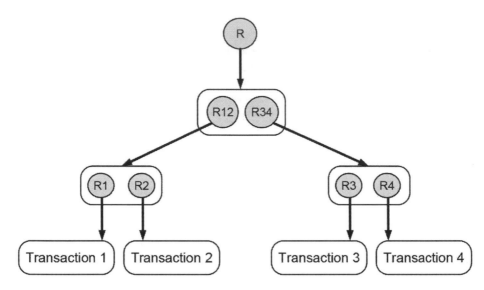

Figure 11-5. Data linked together in a tree-like fashion

Such a structure is also called a Merkle tree[3] because a computer scientist named Merkle proposed it and it looks like a tree that was turn upside down. It is very useful for grouping many distinct pieces of data that are available at the same time and to make them accessible via a single hash reference. In order to create the tree illustrated in Figure 11-5, you start with the four transaction data represented by the boxes at the bottom of the figure. At first the hash references to the individual transaction data are created (R1 to R4), which are grouped together in a pair-wise fashion afterward. Subsequently, hash references to the pairs of hash references are created (R12 and R34). This procedure is repeated until you eventually arrive at a single hash reference, which is also called the root of the Merkle tree (labeled R).

Why It Works

The explained data structures store data in a change-sensitive fashion because they connect and combine data with hash references. These references get broken when the data they refer to are changed after the references were created. Hence, observing a broken reference in such a construct is proof that some of the data were changed after the structure was created. Otherwise, it could be concluded that the whole construct has not been changed since it was created.

---

[3]Merkle, Ralph C. Protocols for Public Key Cryptosystems. *IEEE Symposium on Security and Privacy* 122 (1980).

Causing Time-Consuming Computations

Hash values are not only useful for making basic file operations such as comparing, referring and storing data secure and efficient. Hash values can also be used to allow computers to challenge other computers with elaborate puzzles. While this may sound a bit odd it will turn out that this usage of hash values is one of the most important concept of the blockchain.

The Goal

For reasons that will become understandable in later steps of this book, you may need to create puzzles that require computational resources in order to be solved. It should not be possible to solve these puzzles based on knowledge or data stored somewhere or by means of thinking, like an IQ test or a knowledge test. The only way to solve these puzzle is by sheer computational power and hard computational work.

The Idea

A combination lock is a specific lock that requires a unique sequence of numbers in order for it to be opened. If you do not know the sequence that opens the lock, you would systematically try all possible combinations until you eventually arrived at the unique combination that opens the lock. This procedure is guaranteed to open the lock, but it is time-consuming. Systematically trying all possible combinations has nothing to do with knowledge or intellectual reasoning. The approach of opening a combination lock is based on sheer diligence and hard work. Hash puzzles are computational puzzles that can be seen as the digital equivalent to the task of opening a combination lock by trial and error.

How It Works

Elements of a hash puzzle are[4]:

- Given data that have to be kept unchanged
- Data that can be freely changed, the so-called nonce
- The hash function to be applied
- Restrictions on the hash value of the combined hashing, also called the difficulty level

---

[4]Back, Adam. Hashcash—a denial of service counter-measure. 2002. http://www.hashcash.org/papers/hashcash.pdf.

Figure 11-6 illustrates the setting of the hash puzzle. Combined hashing is applied to the data and the nonce. The resulting hash value has to fulfill the given restrictions.

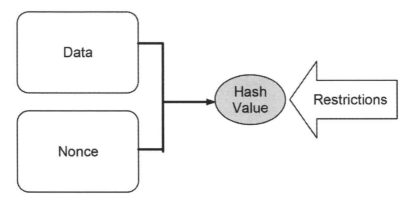

Figure 11-6. Schematic illustration of a hash puzzle

Hash puzzles can only be solved by trial and error. This requires guessing a nonce, calculating the hash value of the combined data with the required hash function, and evaluating the resulting hash value based on the restrictions. If the hash value satisfies the restrictions, you will have solved the hash puzzle; otherwise, you would continue with another nonce until you eventually solve the puzzle. The nonce that, when combined with the given data, yields a hash value that satisfies the restrictions is called the solution. You always have to present that particular nonce when claiming that you solved a hash puzzle.

An Illustrative Example

Let's consider a real hash puzzle for illustrating its functioning. In Step 10 you saw that the shortened hash value of Hello World! is 7F83B165. But what data combined with Hello World! would yield a shortened hash value with three leading zeros? So the hash puzzle is: Find the nonce that combined with Hello World! yields a shortened hash value that starts with three leading zeros.

Let's get our hands dirty and try some nonce. Table 11-1 shows the nonce, the text to be hashed, and the resulting shortened hash value. As you can see, the nonce 614 solves the hash puzzle, which implies that starting with a nonce 0 and incrementing sequentially by 1 you would need 615 steps to find the solution. If the restriction were to find a hash value with one leading zero, you would have solved it already after four steps, since Hello World! 3 yields a hash value with one leading zero.

Table 11-1. Nonces for Solving a Hash Puzzle

Nonce	Text to Be Hashed	Output
0	Hello World! 0	4EE4B774
1	Hello World! 1	3345B9A3
2	Hello World! 2	72040842
3	Hello World! 3	02307D5F
...		
613	Hello World! 613	E861901E
614	Hello World! 614	**00068A3C**
615	Hello World! 615	5EB7483F

You can try this yourself at www.blockchain-basics.com/HashPuzzle.html.

The Difficulty Level

Requiring the hash value to fulfill a certain restriction is the core of the hash puzzle. Hence, neither the restriction nor its description is arbitrary. Instead, the restriction used by hash puzzles is standardized so that computers can challenge other computers with hash puzzles. In the context of hash puzzles, the restrictions are often called *difficulty* or *difficulty level*, respectively. The difficulty is expressed as a natural number and refers to the number of leading zeros the hash value has to have. Hence, a difficulty of 1 means that the hash value has to have (at least) one leading zero, while a difficulty of 10 means that the hash value has to have at least 10 leading zeros. The higher the difficulty level, the more leading zeros are required and the more complicated the hash puzzle is. The more complicated the hash puzzle is, the more computational power or time are needed to solve it.

Why It Works

The functioning of hash puzzles critically depends on the fact that hash functions are one-way functions. It is not possible to solve a hash puzzle by inspecting the restrictions that the hash value has to fulfill and applying the hash function in the opposite direction afterward (i.e., going from the desired output to the required input). Hash puzzles can only be solved by trial and error, which consumes a lot of computing power and hence a lot of time and energy. The level of difficulty directly influences the number of trials needed on average for finding the solution, which in turn influences the computational resources or the time needed to find the solution.

Hash functions are deterministic and quickly produce hash values for any kind of data. Hence, once a solution is found, it is easy to verify that the data combined with the nonce indeed yield a hash value that satisfies the restrictions. If the calculated value does not satisfy the restriction, the hash function cannot be blamed because the deviation is only caused by the fact that the puzzle has not been solved.

■ **Note**   In the context of the blockchain, hash puzzles are often called *proof of work*, as their solution proves that someone has done the work necessary to solve it.

Usage of Hashing in the Blockchain

Within the blockchain, hashing is used in the following instances:

- Storing transaction data in a change-sensitive manner
- As a digital fingerprint of transaction data
- As a way to incur computational costs for changing the blockchain-data-structure

Outlook

This step explained major use cases of hash values and sketched their usage in the blockchain. The next steps will discuss in greater detail the way hashing is utilized by the blockchain.

Summary

- Hash values can be used:
    - To compare data
    - To detect whether data that were supposed to stay unchanged have been altered
    - To refer to data in a change-sensitive manner
    - To store a collection of data in a change-sensitive manner
    - To create computationally expensive tasks

Identifying and Protecting User Accounts

A gentle introduction to cryptography

Besides hash functions, the blockchain uses another base technology exten-sively: asymmetric cryptography. It is the foundation for identifying users in the blockchain and protecting their property. Cryptography is often considered complicated and hard to understand. Hence, this step focuses on introducing cryptography in a gentle way that is easy to comprehend and sufficient for understanding the security concept of the blockchain.

The Metaphor

Long before e-mails, facsimiles, telephones, and chat apps were invented, people used conventional mail to send messages. Along with its modern competitors, conventional mail still exists and is still used by many people. Conventional letters are still delivered by postal employees, who deliver let-ters by putting them in the mailboxes of the addressees. Mailboxes functioning like trapdoors. By design, it is easy to insert a letter through the letter slot, but

© Daniel Drescher 2017
D. Drescher, *Blockchain Basics*, DOI 10.1007/978-1-4842-2604-9_12

it is very hard to pull a letter out that way because taking out letters is supposed to be done only by the addressee who owns the key necessary to open the mailbox. This concept has been used for a very long time and we still use a similar concept when we send an e-mail to an e-mail address, when we send a message in the latest chat app, or when we transfer money to a bank account. In all these cases, the security concept is based on a separation of two kinds of information: first, publicly known information that serves as an address to a trapdoor-like box; and second, private information that serves as the key for opening the box and accessing the things it contains. The blockchain applies the same concept when protecting private data. Hence, keeping this metaphor in mind may provide some guidance on your way in learning about the world of cryptography.

The Goal

The goal is to identify owners and property uniquely and to ensure that only the lawful owner can access his or her property.

The Challenge

The blockchain is a peer-to-peer system that is open to everyone. Everyone can connect and contribute computational resources or submit new transaction data to the system. However, it is not desirable for everyone to access the property assigned to the accounts managed by the blockchain. A constituting characteristic of private property is its exclusiveness. The right to transfer ownership to another account is restricted to the owner of the account who hands off ownership. Hence, the challenge of the blockchain is to protect the property assigned to the accounts without restricting the open architecture of the distributed system.

The Idea

The idea is to treat accounts like mailboxes: everyone can transfer property to it, but only the owner of the account can access the things that are collected inside. The major characteristic of a mailbox is that its location is known and hence anyone can put something in but only the owner can open it with a key. The duality of a public mailbox, on the one hand, and a privately held key, on the other hand, has an equivalent in the digital world: public-private-key encryption. One uses public keys for identifying accounts to which everyone can transfer ownership, while access is restricted to those who possess the corresponding private keys.[1]

A Short Detour to Cryptography

In order to help you understand cryptography, I will discuss the following aspects:

- The major idea of cryptography
- Terminology
- Symmetric cryptography
- Asymmetric cryptography

The Major Idea of Cryptography

The major idea of cryptography is to protect data from being accessed by unauthorized people. It is the digital equivalent to door locks or bank safes, which also protect their content from being accessed by unauthorized people. Similar to locks and keys in the physical world, cryptography also uses keys to protect data.

Terminology[2]

The digital equivalent to closing a lock is encryption, while the digital equivalent to opening a lock is decryption. Hence, when talking about protecting data by using cryptography, we use the terms encryption and decryption for protecting data and unprotecting data, respectively. Encrypted data are called cypher text. Cypher text looks like a useless pile of letters and figures to everyone who does not know how to decrypt it. However, cypher text is indeed useful but only for those who possess the key necessary to decrypt it. Decrypted cypher text is identical to the original data that have been encrypted. Hence, the whole round trip through cryptography can be summed up as: start with some data, produce cypher text by encrypting the original data with a cryptographic key, preserve the cypher text or send it to someone, and finally recover the original data by decrypting the cypher text with a cryptographic key. Figure 12-1 illustrates the basic functioning of cryptography.

---

[1]Nakamoto, Satoshi. Bitcoin: A peer-to-peer electronic cash system. 2008. https://bitcoin.org/bitcoin.pdf.
[2]See Van Tilborg, Henk, and Sushil Jajodia, eds. *Encyclopedia of cryptography and security*. New York: Springer Science & Business Media, 2014.

Figure 12-1. Schematic illustration of basic cryptographic concepts and their terminology

What happens if someone tries to decrypt cypher text by using an incorrect key? The result is a useless pile of numbers, letters, and signs that do not reveal any of the data that were encrypted.

Symmetric Cryptography

For many years people utilized methods of cryptography where the identical key was used to do both the encrypting and decrypting of data. Hence, everyone who was able to encrypt data with such a key was automatically able to decrypt cypher text created with that key as well. Since the identical key was used for both methods, this was called symmetric cryptography. Figure 12-2 illustrates the basic functioning of symmetric cryptography where the identical key is used to encrypt and to decrypt a short greeting.

Figure 12-2. Schematic illustration of symmetric cryptography

However, it turned out that having one key for encryption and decryption was not always desirable. As a result, asymmetric cryptography was invented.

Asymmetric Cryptography

Asymmetric cryptography always uses two complementary keys. But there is a trick to this: cypher text created with one of these keys can only be decrypted with the other key and vice versa.

Figure 12-3 illustrates the encryption-decryption round trip for asymmetric cryptography. You can view this figure in the following way: The upper part of Figure 12-3 illustrates encryption, while the lower part illustrates decryption.

There are two keys: a white key and a black key. Together they form the pair of corresponding keys. The original message is encrypted with the black key, which yields cypher text represented by the black box containing white letters. The original message can also be encrypted with the second key, which yields different cypher text represented by the white box containing black letters. For didactical reasons, the colors of the boxes representing cypher text and the colors of the keys used to produce them are identical in order to highlight their relation: The black key yields black cypher text, while the white key produces white cypher text.

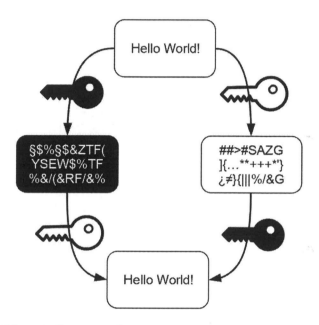

Figure 12-3. Schematic illustration of asymmetric cryptography

The lower part of Figure 12-3 illustrates how decryption works in asymmetric cryptography. Black cypher text can only be decrypted with the white key and vice versa.

The trick to asymmetric cryptography is that you can never decrypt cypher text with the key that was used to create it. The decision on which key to use for encryption and which to use for decryption is up to you. You can switch the roles of the keys as you like for every new piece of data you want to encrypt, but you always have to keep both keys for doing both encryption and decryption. If you have only one of the keys, your power is limited. While you can always create cypher text by applying your key to data, you cannot decrypt it because you are missing the complementary key. However, you can decrypt cypher text that was created with the corresponding complementary key. An isolated key is like a one-way street: You can drive down the street but you can never drive back on the identical street. Due to the asymmetric distribution of their cryptographic power, the two keys allow you to separate the group of people who are able to create cypher text from those who can decrypt it.

Asymmetric Cryptography in the Real World

Using asymmetric cryptography in real life consists of two major steps:

- Creating and distributing the keys
- Using the keys

Creating and Distributing the Keys

When using asymmetric cryptography in real life, you would give the two keys specific names in order to highlight each one's role. Typically these keys are called the private key and public key. For that reason, asymmetric cryptography is called public-private-key cryptography. However, there are no such things as the private key and public key in asymmetric cryptography per se because you know that you can encrypt data and decrypt cypher text with each of them. It is the role that is assigned to these keys that makes them private or public. The public key is given to everyone, regardless of their trustworthiness. Literally anyone can have a copy of the public key. However, the private key is kept safe and private.

Hence, the first steps to be performed in any application of asymmetric cryptography are:

1. Create a pair of complementary keys by using cryptographic software

2. Give one key the name public key

3. Give the other key the name private key

4. Keep the private key for yourself

5. Give your public key to everyone else

Using the Keys

There are two general ways to use the pair of keys, which differ in the direction to which the data flows:

- Public to private
- Private to public

Public to Private

By using the keys in this way, the information flows from the public key, where it is encrypted, to the private key, where it is decrypted. This usage of the two complementary keys is similar to a mailbox, where everyone can put letters in but only the owner can open it. It is the straightforward usage of asymmetric cryptography because it fits our intuition about privacy and publicity in the same way as our address and our mailbox is public but its content is private. Hence, this way of using asymmetric cryptography is all about sending information in a secured fashion to the owner of the private key. It works because everyone can create cypher text with the public key, but only the owner of the private key can decrypt the cypher text and read the message.

Private to Public

By using the keys in this way, the information flows from the private key, where it is encrypted, to the public key, where it is decrypted. This way of using the two keys is similar to a public news board or public notice board where everyone who has a copy of the public key can read messages but only the owner of the private key can create messages. Hence, this way of using asymmetric cryptography is all about proving authorship. It works because everyone can use the public key to decrypt cypher text that was created with the corresponding private key. The fact that cypher text created with the private key can only be decrypted with the corresponding public key serves as proof that the owner of the corresponding private key has encrypted the message.

Asymmetric Cryptography in the Blockchain

The blockchain uses asymmetric cryptography in order to achieve two goals:

- Identifying accounts
- Authorizing transactions

Identifying Accounts

The blockchain needs to identify users or user accounts, respectively, in order to maintain the mapping between owner and property. The blockchain uses the public-to-private approach of asymmetric cryptography for identifying user accounts and transferring ownership between them. Account numbers in the blockchain are actually public cryptographic keys. Hence, transaction data use the public cryptographic keys for identifying the accounts involved in the transfer of ownership. In this regard, the blockchain treats user accounts similar to mailboxes: They have a publicly known address and everyone is able to send messages to them.

Authorizing Transactions

Transaction data always have to include a piece of data that serves as proof that the owner of the account who hands off ownership indeed agrees with the described transfer of ownership. The flow of information implied by this agreement starts at the owner of the account who hands off ownership and is supposed to reach everyone who inspects the transaction data. This kind of information flow is similar to that implied by the private-to-public use case of asymmetric cryptography. The owner of the account who hands off ownership creates some cypher text with his or her private key. All others can verify this proof of agreement by using the public cryptographic key, which happens to be the number of the account that hands off ownership. The details of this procedure, which is called digital signature, will be explained in more detail in the next step.

Outlook

This step explained the concept of asymmetric cryptography and how it is used as public-private-key cryptography in real life. Furthermore, this step explained that cryptographic public keys are used in the blockchain to identify user accounts. Furthermore, the lawful owner authorizes transactions by creating a digital signature that can be traced back to his or her private cryptographic key. The next step explains this concept in more detail, as this usage of asymmetric cryptography is less intuitive than the identification of accounts by public keys.

Summary

- The major goal of cryptography is to protect data from being accessed by unauthorized people.

- The major cryptographic activities are:

  - Encryption: Protecting data by turning them into cypher text by utilizing a cryptographic key

  - Decryption: Turning cypher text back into useful data by utilizing a matching cryptographic key

- Asymmetric cryptography always uses two complementary keys: cypher text created with one of these keys can only be decrypted with the other key and vice versa.

- When utilizing asymmetric cryptography in real life, these keys are typically called the public key and private key in order to highlight their role. The public key is shared with everyone, while the private key is kept secret. For this reason, asymmetric cryptography is also called public-private-key cryptography.

- There are two classical use cases of public and private keys:

  - Everyone uses the public key to encrypt data that can only be decrypted by the owner of the corresponding private key. This is the digital equivalent to a public mailbox where everyone can put letters in but only the owner can open it.

  - The owner of the private key uses it to encrypt data that can be decrypted by everyone who possesses the corresponding public key. This is the digital equivalent to a public notice board that proves authorship.

- The blockchain uses asymmetric cryptography in order to achieve two goals:

  - Identifying accounts: User accounts are public cryptographic keys.

  - Authorizing transactions: The owner of the account who hands off ownership creates a piece of cypher text with the corresponding private key. This piece of cypher text can be verified by using the corresponding public key, which happens to be the number of the account that hands off ownership.

Authorizing Transactions

Utilizing the digital equivalent to handwritten signatures

Step 12 provided a gentle introduction to asymmetric cryptography. It also pointed out that the blockchain uses public cryptographic keys as account numbers and utilizes the public-to-private approach of asymmetric cryptography for transferring ownership among accounts. However, that was only half of the story. The blockchain needs to ensure that only the lawful owner can transfer his or her property to other accounts. This is the point were the concept of authorization enters the scene. Hence, this step explains how asymmetric cryptography is used within the blockchain for authorizing transactions. In particular, this step is devoted to the concept of digital signatures, which utilize the private-to-public approach of asymmetric cryptography.

The Metaphor

Handwritten signatures serve an important purpose: they state agreement with the content of a document and agree with its execution. The reason why we accept handwritten signatures as evidence for agreement is the uniqueness of each person's handwriting. Every human being has his or her own characteristic

© Daniel Drescher 2017

D. Drescher, *Blockchain Basics*, DOI 10.1007/978-1-4842-2604-9_13

way of writing his or her name. Hence, when we identify a name being written in a specific way, we conclude that the person who writes his or her name in that particular way has indeed produced that handwritten signature, and, as a result, we can conclude that this person has agreed with the content of the document and its implementation. This step explains the concept of stating agreement with transactions in an electronic ledger that is similar to handwritten signatures. This concept is crucial for the security of individual transactions in the blockchain.

The Goal

It is important to ensure that only the owner of an account can transfer the property associated with it to other accounts. Every attempt to access an account and its associated property by any person other than the lawful owner should be identified as unauthorized and should be rejected.

The Challenge

The peer-to-peer system under consideration is open to everyone. Hence, everyone may create transactions and can submit them to the system. Transaction data are the foundation of describing and clarifying ownership. Only the lawful owner of an account should be able to transfer property or ownership rights associated with his or her account to another account. The challenge of the blockchain is to maintain its openness while restricting the transfer of ownership to the lawful owner.

The Idea

The main idea of ensuring that only the lawful owner can transfer ownership is to utilize a digital security measure that is equivalent to handwritten signatures and serves the same purpose: identifying an account, stating the agreement of its owner with the content of specific transaction data, and approving its execution by allowing the data to be added to the history of transaction data.

A Short Detour to Digital Signatures

Digital signatures are the equivalent of handwritten signatures. They utilize cryptographic hashing and the private-to-public information flow of asymmetric cryptography. The following short example illustrates the three major elements of digital signatures:

- Creating a signature
- Verifying data by using the signature
- Identifying fraud by using the signature

Creating a Signature

Let's say I want to send a Hello World! greeting to the world in an authorized way. Hence, I create a message that contains the greeting and a corresponding digital signature. Figure 13-1 depicts the whole process of signing data digitally. The process starts with the white box in the top left area of Figure 13-1 that contains the greeting. I create the hash value of the greeting, which is 7F83B165, and encrypt it with my private key. The cypher text of the greeting's hash value (the black box containing white letters) is my digital signature of the greeting. It is unique with respect to two aspects: First, it can be traced back to me uniquely because I created it with my unique private key. Second, it is unique regarding the text of the greeting because it is based on the digital fingerprint of the greeting. Both the greeting and the digital signature are put together in a file (the gray box), which is my digitally signed message to the world.

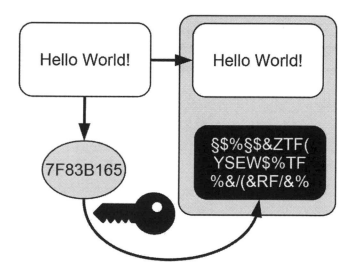

Figure 13-1. Schematic illustration of creating a digital signature

Verifying Data by Using the Signature

The message, that is, my greeting together with the digital signature, is sent to the whole world. Everyone can verify that I authorized this message by utilizing my public key. Figure 13-2 illustrates the process of verifying the message by using the digital signature. The process starts with the greeting. At first the recipient of the message calculates the hash value of the greeting by himself, which yields the value 7F83B165. Then the recipient of my message decrypts the attached cypher text (the digital signature) with my public key. Doing so yields the value 7F83B165, which is the hash value of that version of the greeting I wanted to send to the world. Comparing both hash values completes the verification. Since both hash values are identical, the recipient correctly concludes, first, that the message was signed by me, because he was able to decrypt the signature with my public key, and second, that the greeting text found in the message is indeed the one I wanted to send because the decrypted cypher text is identical with the hash value of the greeting in the message.

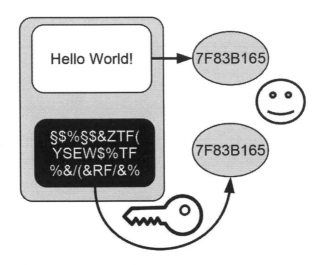

Figure 13-2. Using a digital signature to verify a message

Identifying Fraud by Using the Signature

Figure 13-3 illustrates how the digital signature points out a forged greeting.

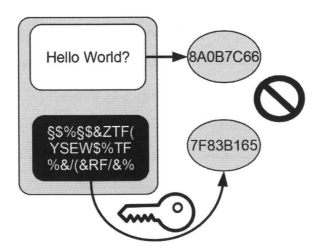

Figure 13-3. Using a digital signature to identify fraud

Figure 13-3 shows the message that arrived in my friend's mailbox. Note the change of the greeting text. Some hacker replaced the exclamation mark with a question mark and hence changed the whole tone of the greeting. This is not the way I wanted to greet the world. Fortunately, the digital signature will point out to everyone that the message has been altered against my will.

At first the recipient of the message will create the hash value of the greeting by himself, which yields the value 8A0B7C66. Then the recipient of my message decrypts the digital signature with my public key. Doing so yields 7F83B165, which is the hash value of the version of the greeting I wanted to send to the world. Comparing both hash values reveals that they are not identical. This clearly points out that the greeting in the message is not the greeting I wanted to send to the world. Hence, everyone concludes that I did not authorize this message, and, therefore, no one will make me responsible for its content.

How It Works

Digital signatures in the blockchain fulfill the following requirements:

- They state agreement of the owner of the account who hands off ownership with specific transaction data.

- They are unique for the whole content of transaction data in order to prevent it from being used to authorize other transactions without the agreement of its author.

- Only the owner of the account who hands off ownership can create such a signature.

- They are easy to verify by everyone.

There are two use cases of digital signatures in the blockchain:

- Signing a transaction
- Verifying a transaction

Signing a Transaction

In order to create a digital signature for a transaction, the owner of the account who hands off ownership performs the following steps:

1. Describes the transaction with all necessary information such as the involved account numbers, amount being transferred, and so on except the signature itself as it is not yet available.

2. Create the cryptographic hash value of the transaction data.

3. Encrypt the hash value of the transaction with the private key of the account that hands off ownership.

4. Add the cypher text created in point 3 to the transaction as its digital signature.

Verifying a Transaction

In order to verify a transaction, the following steps must be performed:

1. Create the hash value of the transaction data to be verified except the signature itself.

2. Decrypt the digital signature of the transaction under consideration with the account number that hands off ownership.

3. Compare the hash value of step 1 with the value gained in step 2. If both are identical, the transaction is authorized by the owner of the private key that corresponds to the account that hands off ownership, otherwise it is not.

Why It Works

Digital signatures of transaction data are a combination of the following:

- Cryptographic hash values of transaction data

- Cypher text that can be traced back to the corresponding private key of an account

Due to the fact that cryptographic hash values can be considered digital fingerprints, they are unique for each transaction. A constituting property of public-private-key cryptography is that cypher text created with one key can only be decrypted with the corresponding key. The association of both keys is unique. Hence, a successful decryption of cypher text with a specific public key serves as proof that it was created with the corresponding private key. Both concepts combined are used to create cypher text that can be traced back uniquely to one specific transaction data and to one specific private key in one process. This property make digital signatures suitable to serve as proof that the owner of the private key that was used to create the digital signature indeed agrees with the content of the transaction.

Outlook

This step completes the process of how the blockchain protects ownership on the level of individual transaction data. As a result, transactions and their purpose to transfer and prove ownership are safe and secure. However, it is important to ensure that transaction data are not only secured on the individual level. There is still a need to store the whole history of transaction data in a secure way. The next steps will explain in more detail how to achieve this.

Summary

- Handwritten signatures on documents state the agreement of their authors with the content of the signed documents and authorize their implementation.

- The evidential power of handwritten signatures is based on the uniqueness of the handwriting.

- Digital signatures are the digital equivalent to handwritten signatures.

- Digital signatures serve two purposes:

  - Identify its author uniquely

  - State agreement of its author with the content of a document and authorize its execution

- In the blockchain, digital signatures of transactions are cryptographic hash values of transaction data encrypted with the private key that corresponds to the account that hands off ownership.

- Digital signatures in the blockchain can be trace back uniquely to one specific private key and to one specific transaction in one process.

Storing Transaction Data

Building and maintaining a history of transaction data

Based on the previous five steps, you should now be able to trace ownership based on the whole history of transaction data and to describe individual transfers of ownership in a secure way by authorizing transactions with digital signatures and identifying user accounts uniquely. However, I have not spent any time discussing how to store all the transaction data that make up the transaction history in a secure fashion. This is the point where the block-chain-data-structure enters the discussion. This step introduces the block-chain-data-structure and explains how it is constructed.

© Daniel Drescher 2017
D. Drescher, *Blockchain Basics*, DOI 10.1007/978-1-4842-2604-9_14

The Metaphor

Do you remember the last time you visited a library and used one of the traditional card catalogs? Library catalogs are registers of all of the books owned by a library. Some traditional libraries still use card catalogs for managing their inventory. Each card in one of these catalogs represents one book, and the card displays the major information about that book, such as the name of the author, the title of the book, the date of publication, and the location of the book within the library such as floor, room, shelf, and rack number. In order to identify books, the catalog cards often contain unique reference numbers that are also displayed on the books' spines. Most libraries maintain more than one card catalog, which differ with respect to the criterion used to order the cards. For example, in an author catalog, the cards are sorted alphabetically according to the names of authors, while in a title catalog the cards are sorted alphabetically according to the titles. One could also come up with an ordering catalog whose cards are sorted according the order in which the books where added to the library. This step explains how the blockchain stores transaction data in a way that is similar to a library with an ordering catalog.

The Goal

The goal of the blockchain is to maintain the whole history of transaction data in an ordered fashion.

The Challenge

The challenge is to store all transaction data that have ever happened in a way that preserves the order in which the transactions happened and in a way that quickly and easily detects any changes made to the data. Detecting changes quickly is important since it is the basis to prevent manipulation or forgery of the transaction history.

The Idea

The idea is to create a library of transaction data and to maintain an ordering catalog, which preserves the order in which transactions were added to the library. In order to detect any changes made either to the ordering catalog or to the individual transaction data, the data must be stored in a change-sensitive manner by using hash references.

Transforming a Book into a Blockchain-Data-Structure

This section explains how to turn a book into a small library with an ordering catalog, which turns out to be a simplified version of the blockchain-data-structure.

Starting Point: A Book

For many centuries, written information was preserved on unwieldy spools of parchment, which were called scrolls. Nowadays, we are used to having written information preserved in codices: hardback-bound bundles of numbered pages, which we call books. Because books are so commonplace, we may take their innovation for granted. Some of their important properties include:

- Storing content: Books store content on their pages.

- Ordering: The sentences on the pages as well as the pages within the book are kept in order.

- Connecting pages: Pages are physically connected via the book spine and logically connected via their content and the page numbers.

As a result of these properties, we can browse through books forward and backward by moving pages or we can jump directly to specific pages by utilizing the page numbers. Let's see what we could achieve if we changed some of these properties.

Transformation 1: Making Page Dependency Explicit

Figure 14-1 exhibits a schematic illustration of two pages from a very simple book. Each page contains a top margin that presents the page number and a content area that carries only one word.

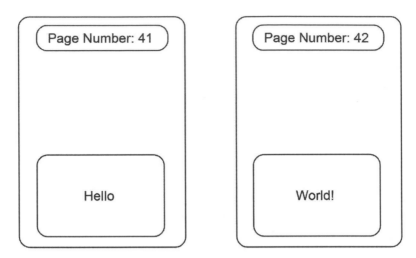

Figure 14-1. A schematic illustration of book pages

The page numbers serve an important purpose: You can find out whether someone removed a page from the book by verifying that the page numbers continue without leaving out a number. Imagine you are currently reading page number 42 of our simplified book. What page number should the preceding page have? This is very simple: The preceding page should have the number 41, which equals 42 minus 1. In order to verify that indeed no one has removed the preceding page, we compare the number being displayed on the preceding page with the expected page number, which is the number of the current page minus 1. If both numbers are equal, we can conclude that the preceding page has not been removed.

Why do we know that the number of the preceding page should equal the current page's number minus 1? The answer is that we assume that all books follow the convention of labeling the pages consecutively with natural numbers. But what if that assumption is not true because the author or the publisher of the book decided to use a different page numbering schema (e.g., by only using even numbers or multiples of three)? In this case, our approach of verifying that the preceding page has not been removed fails. In order to make it easy to verify that no page has been removed from the book, we could point out the connection of each page to its predecessor explicitly. Figure 14-2 shows how this is done in our simple book. Each page not only exhibits its own number but also exhibits the number of its preceding page. This page numbering schema makes the dependency between any page and its preceding page explicit. The explicit referencing of the preceding page makes verifying that no page has been removed very easy since it does not rely on implicit assumptions anymore.

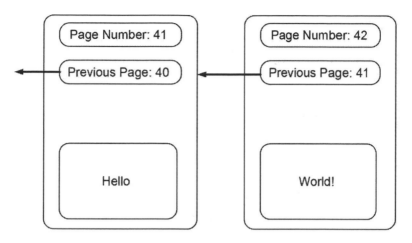

Figure 14-2. Book pages with explicit reference to their preceding pages

Transformation 2: Outsourcing the Content

The pages of our book contain the content and the information necessary to maintain their ordering: the page numbers. We can make our book handier by outsourcing the content and let it solely focus on the task of maintaining the order. Figure 14-3 shows how the pages of our schematic book look after we outsourced the content. The pages no longer contain any content, instead they contain reference numbers that point to the content, which can be stored wherever we want (e.g., in a box, on a shelf, or somewhere else).

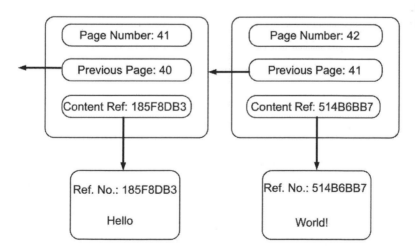

Figure 14-3. Book pages with reference values to the outsourced content

The achievement of this step is the following: We turned our book into a small library. The book that once stored content and page numbers together has been turned into a catalog, whose sole purpose is maintaining the order of the content while the content is stored on separated pages that are identified by unique reference numbers.

Transformation 3: Replacing Page Numbers

Our book that is now an ordering catalog maintains the order of its pages in two distinct ways: First, by the physical location of the pages within the book fixated in the book spine; second, by the page numbers and the explicit referencing of the preceding page. Due to the fact that the physical construction of the book preserves the order of the pages, we can experiment with a different page numbering schema. We can actually replace the natural numbers used to label the pages with reference numbers. Figure 14-4 shows the result of this transformation. For example, the page previously carrying the page number 42 is now identified with the page reference number 8118E736. In a similar fashion, the page that previously carried the page number 41 is now identified with the page reference number B779E800. Notice that the references to the preceding page have been updated as well. The page with the reference number 8118E736 contains the correct reference number to its preceding page.

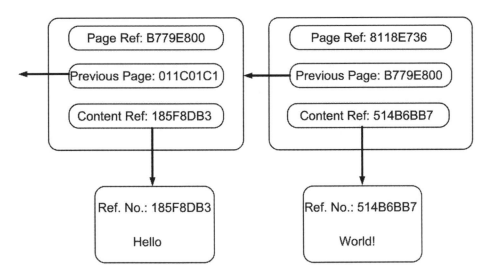

Figure 14-4. Book pages using reference numbers as page numbers

Transformation 4: Creating Reference Numbers

In the previous transformation, we replaced page numbers in our book with reference numbers. However, I have not discussed how they would be created. The best way to create unique reference numbers is to use cryptographic hash values. Hence, we can identify pages in our catalog as well as the corresponding content pages with their cryptographic hash values, which are digital fingerprints of their content. For simplicity, both Figure 14-3 and Figure 14-4 use shortened hash values. (You can verify the results by using the tool provided at `www.blockchain-basics.com/Hashing.html`.) For example, the content page that contains the word Hello is identified by the shortened hash value of Hello that is 185F8DB3. The reference value of our book pages are calculated based on their content, which is the content reference number and the reference number of the preceding page. For example, the page reference number B779E800 is the hash value of 011C01C1 185F8DB3.

Transformation 5: Getting Rid of the Book Spine

Our ordering catalog is an unusual book because each of its pages contains its own reference number, the reference number of the preceding page, and the reference number of the corresponding content page. However, our ordering catalog is still a traditional book whose pages are fixated in the book spine.

What happens if we get rid of the book spine and turn our ordering book into a pile of loose pages? By doing so we destroy the physical connection of the pages and as a result we lose the physical ordering of our pages as well. Fortunately, the ordering of the pages is not completely lost. Every page contains the reference number of its preceding page. As a result, we can move from page to page backward by following the page reference numbers to the preceding page. If we keep the last page of the ordering catalog separated, we can always browse through all pages in reverse order.

Goal Achieved: Appreciating the Result

Let's summarize what we have achieved in this example. We turned a classical book into two physically unordered piles of loose pages that are linked together with unique reference numbers. One pile of pages contains the content, while the other pile of pages maintains the ordering. For simplicity, we refer to the latter pile of pages as an ordering catalog. Each page of the ordering catalog contains the reference number to its preceding page and the reference number of the corresponding content page. As a result, we have separated ordering from storing information and the logical location (the order) from the physical location of the pages. Due to the fact that we used hash values as reference numbers, everyone can verify their correctness by simply recalculating them. Since the pages of the ordering catalog are no longer fixated on a book spine, we can only browse through it backward in a page-by-page fashion by following the page reference numbers that point to the preceding page. For easy reference, Table 14-1 summarizes the properties of our book before and after the transformations.

Table 14-1. Comparing the Book Before and After the Transformation

Property	Book	Transformed Book
Storing content	On the pages themselves	On separate content pages Each content page is identified by a unique reference number
Ordering content	Physically: Based on the location of the pages within the book Logically: Based on the page numbers	Logically: Via an ordering catalog that contains reference values to the content pages
Connecting pages	Physically: By fixating pages in the book spine Logically: Based on page numbers	Logically: Via reference numbers
Browsing through the pages	Forward Backward Jumping to pages directly by using page numbers	Backward only: By following the reference numbers to the preceding page

The Blockchain-Data-Structure

What is the blockchain-data-structure? Actually, you already know the answer because the preceding example developed a simplified blockchain-data-structure. However, we used different terminology. This section finishes the analogy by linking the elements of the transformed book with the terminology used in the context of the blockchain.

Our transformed book consists of:

- A mental unit consisting of a page of the ordering catalog and its corresponding content page
- A pile of loose pages called the ordering catalog
- A pile of loose pages that contain the content
- Page reference numbers for identifying and linking pages of the ordering catalog
- Content reference numbers for identifying and linking content pages

For easy reference Table 14-2 at the end of this section summarizes the results by comparing the elements of our simplified book after transformation with elements of the blockchain-data-structure.

Table 14-2. Comparing the Transformed Book with the Blockchain-Data-Structure

Transformed Book	Blockchain-Data-Structure[1]
A page in the ordering catalog	A block header
The whole ordering catalog	The chain of block headers
The reference number of a page in the ordering catalog	The cryptographic hash value of a block header
The reference number to the preceding page	The cryptographic hash value of the preceding block header
Content	Transaction data
A content page	A Merkle tree containing transaction data
Reference to the content page	The root of the Merkle tree that contains transaction data
The mental unit of a page of the ordering catalog and its corresponding content page	One block of the blockchain-data-structure
The whole ordering catalog and all content pages together	The blockchain-data-structure

The Mental Unit of a Page of the Ordering Catalog and Its Corresponding Content Page

The mental unit of a page of the ordering catalog and its corresponding content page relates to one block in the blockchain-data-structure. All these blocks together form the blockchain-data-structure. It is important to point out that the unit of ordering page and corresponding content page is only a mental unit because the pages of the ordering catalog and the content pages are physically distinct entities. The former refer to the latter via hash references, which as a result constitutes the mental unity.

Ordering Catalog

The ordering catalog of our transformed book equates to the chain of block headers in the blockchain-data-structure. Each page of the ordering catalog equates to a single block header in the blockchain-data-structure. Since the

---

[1]Nakamoto, Satoshi. Bitcoin: A peer-to-peer electronic cash system. 2008. https://bitcoin.org/bitcoin.pdf.

block headers are connected with one another via references in a linear fashion, like the links of a chain, they form a chain of block headers. Similar to our ordering catalog, the chain of block headers does not store transaction data directly, but only stores hash references to the corresponding transaction data. This is the point where the mental unit of the ordering catalog and content becomes important.

Content Pages

The content of the transformed book is equivalent to the transaction data being maintained by the blockchain. They are specific to our application area that is managing ownership. There are no content pages in real-world blockchain applications; I made up the term content pages for didactical reasons. Real-world blockchain applications store the content data (e.g., transaction data) directly in a database, and we refer to them as Merkle trees, whose roots are stored in block headers.

Catalog Page Reference Numbers

The page reference numbers of our transformed book used to identify pages of the ordering catalog equate to cryptographic hash values of individual block headers in the blockchain-data-structure. They are called block hash or previous block's hash, respectively. They are used to identify each block header uniquely and to refer to the previous block header. The actual referencing from one block header to its predecessor is done by hash reference.

Content Reference Numbers

The content reference numbers in our transformed book used to identify content pages equate to hash references in the chain of block headers that point to the associated transaction data. To be more specific, the content reference number that is stored in a block header is the root of a Merkle tree of the transaction data being stored in a database. This is the point where the mental unit of the ordering catalog (block header) and its corresponding content (Merkle tree with transaction data) are constituted.

Storing Transactions in the Blockchain-Data-Structure

Figure 14-5 summarizes what you have learned by schematically depicting a blockchain-data-structure that stores four transactions. The illustration given in Figure 14-5 shows a simplified blockchain-data-structure that consists of two blocks labeled BLOCK 1 and BLOCK 2. In order to emphasize the mental nature of the blocks, they are drawn with dashed lines. Both blocks contain block headers labeled Block Header 1 and Block Header 2, respectively. BLOCK 1 is the very first block in this data structure, hence, it does not have a preceding block, and, consequently, Block Header 1 does not contain any reference to a preceding block header. Since BLOCK 2 has a predecessor, Block Header 2 maintains a hash reference to its preceding block header labeled as B1. The depicted blockchain-data-structure maintains hash reference to two distinct Merkle trees whose roots are labeled R12 and R34, respectively. The labels of the Merkle roots already give us an indication of the transaction data they contain (e.g., the Merkle tree with the root R12 contains the first two transactions labeled as Transaction 1 and Transaction 2 and their corresponding hash references R1 and R2 that point to them).

If you joined a distributed peer-to-peer system that maintained a blockchain-data-structure, as shown in Figure 14-5, you would receive all transaction data, all hash reference values, and all block headers. Based on these data, your local computer would create the blockchain-data-structure including the hash references that point to data stored on your local computer. Equipped with these data and the reference to the most current block header, you could browse through the history of all transaction data that were ever submitted to the system since its creation in reverse order, which in our case is just four transactions. Note that the reference to the most currently added block header is called the **head** of the blockchain-data-structure because it is the place where the next block will be added. Sometimes both the most currently added block header and the reference that points to it is called the head of the blockchain-data-structure. In Figure 14-5 the reference labeled B2 is the head of the blockchain-data-structure. It is important not to mix the terms "head" and "header": The blockchain-data-structure consists of many blocks that each has its own header, but the whole blockchain-data-structure has only one head.

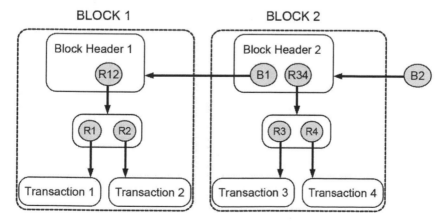

Figure 14-5. A simplified blockchain-data-structure containing four transactions

---

▓ **Caution** The blockchain-data-structure discussed in this step and illustrated in Figure 14-5 has been simplified for didactical reasons. Many details regarding the information stored in the block headers have been left out deliberately. Some of them will be covered in the next steps as you complete your understanding of the blockchain.

Outlook

This step introduced the blockchain-data-structure and explained its construction. The way in which the blockchain-data-structure makes extensive use of hash references makes it a very change-sensitive data store. The next step explains that property in more detail, as it is the key to understanding how the blockchain is made secure.

Summary

- The blockchain-data-structure is a specific kind of data structure that is made up of ordered units called blocks.

- Each block of the blockchain-data-structure consists of a block header and a Merkle tree that contains transaction data.

- The blockchain-data-structure consists of two major data structures: an ordered chain of block headers and Merkle trees.

- One can imagine the ordered chain of block headers as being the digital equivalent to an old-fashioned library card catalog, where the individual catalog cards are sorted according to the order in which they were added to the catalog.

- Having each block header referencing its preceding block header preserves the order of the individual block headers and blocks, respectively, that make up the blockchain-data-structure.

- Each block header in the blockchain-data-structure is identified by its cryptographic hash value and contains a hash reference to its preceding block header and a hash reference to the application-specific data whose order it maintains.

- The hash reference to the application-specific data is typically the root of a Merkle tree that maintains hash references to the application-specific data.

Using the Data Store

Chaining blocks of data

Step 14 introduced the blockchain-data-structure. It turns out that the block-chain-data-structure consists of two major components: an ordered chain of block headers and Merkle trees containing transaction data. This data structure was invented with the goal of storing transaction data in a secure fashion. But what does storing data in a secure fashion mean in this context? Answering this question is the purpose of this step. This step points out the consequences of changing data in the blockchain and it illustrates how the blockchain-data-structure detects changes. Furthermore, this step highlights the power of hash references when storing data in a change-sensitive manner. Finally, this step explains how to add new blocks to the blockchain-data-structure in a correct way.

The Metaphor

Knitting is the craft of turning yarn into a textile or fabric by creating a sequence of multiple interlocking loops of yarn, the so-called stitches. When produced manually, the sizes of knitting stitches vary significantly. Hence, during the process of knitting, it is sometimes necessary to correct individual stitches. In order to correct a knitting stitch located somewhere in the fabric, one has

© Daniel Drescher 2017
D. Drescher, *Blockchain Basics*, DOI 10.1007/978-1-4842-2604-9_15

to rip out all of its succeeding stitches in reverse order starting from the end of the row until one eventually arrives at the stitch to be corrected. After the stitch under consideration has been corrected, one has to re-create all its succeeding stitches. Since this procedure is quite elaborate, it is important to ensure that all stitches fulfill the quality requirements when they are created the first time. This step explains that using the blockchain-data-structure is very similar to knitting: Adding a new block at the end of the blockchain-data-structure is easy, while changing data located somewhere in the chain is quite elaborate. With this metaphor in mind, you should easily be able to understand how the blockchain-data-structure detects changes, on the one hand, and how data are added and changed correctly, on the other hand.

Adding New Transactions

In order to understand how to add new transactions to an existing blockchain-data-structure in an orderly way, let's consider a simple example. Figure 15-1 illustrates the initial situation of a blockchain-data-structure that consist of one block only. The existing blockchain-data-structure only maintains two transactions. Transaction 3 and Transaction 4 at the bottom of Figure 15-1 are not yet added to the blockchain-data-structure. The steps to be performed in order to add new transaction data are:

1. Create a new Merkle tree that contains all new transaction data to be added, as shown in Figure 15-2.

2. Create a new block header (Block Header 2) that contains both the hash reference (B1) that points to the header of its preceeding block (Block Header 1) and the root of the Merkle tree that contains the new transaction data (R34), as shown in Figure 15-3.

3. Create a new hash reference (B2) to the new block header, as shown in Figure 15-4, and declare it the the new **head** of the updated blockchain-data-structure. Remember that the reference that points to the most currently added piece of data in a chain is also called the **head** of the whole chain (see Step 11).

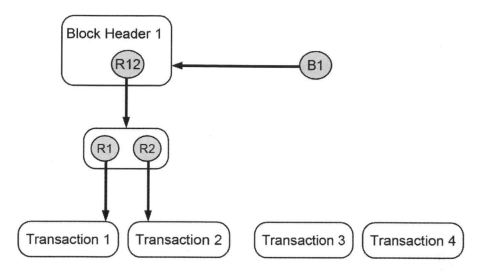

Figure 15-1. Initial situation: Two new transactions (Transaction 3 and Transaction 4) should be added to the existing blockchain-data-structure

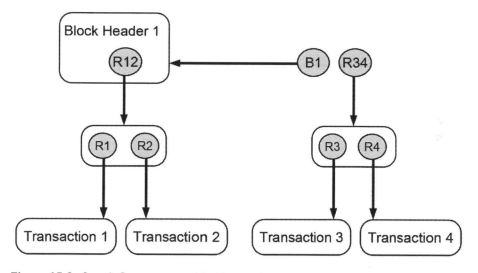

Figure 15-2. Step 1: Creating a new Merkle tree that contains the new transactions

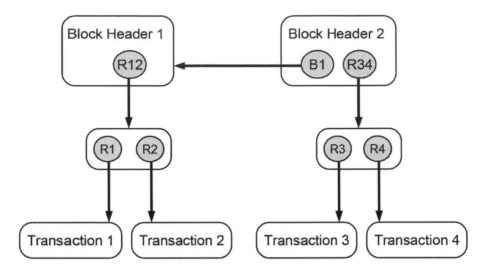

Figure 15-3. Step 2: Create a new block header that contains both the hash reference to its preceding header and the root of the Merkle tree that contains the new transaction data

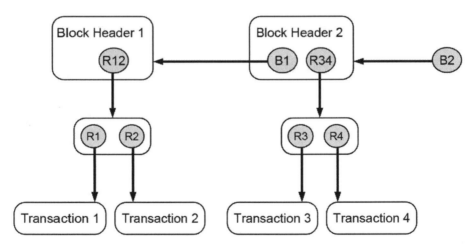

Figure 15-4. Step 3: Create a new hash reference that points to the new block header, which is now the new head of the whole updated blockchain-data-structure

Detecting Changes

The step depicted in Figure 15-4 serves as the initial situation for studying the impact of changing data that are already part of the blockchain-data-structure. I will discuss the following cases:

- Changing the content of transaction data
- Changing a reference in the Merkle tree
- Replacing a transaction
- Changing the Merkle root
- Changing a block header reference

Changing the Content of Transaction Data

Figure 15-5 illustrates what happens if we change Transaction 2. This transaction is part of a Merkle tree, which consists of hash references. By changing some properties of the Transaction 2 (e.g., the amount of goods being transferred or the account that receives ownership), one also changes its fingerprint or its cryptographic hash value, respectively. As a result, the hash reference R2 that pointed to the original transaction data is broken. It detects that the transaction data it originally referred were changed in the meantime and hence violates the rules of staying unchanged. As a result, the whole blockchain-data-structure is invalid.

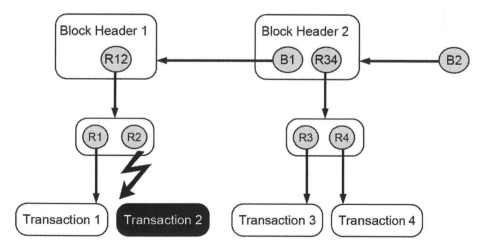

Figure 15-5. Changing the details of a transaction invalidates the hash reference that pointed to the original data, which invalidates the whole data structure

Changing a Reference in the Merkle Tree

Figure 15-6 illustrates what happens if one not only changes details of a transaction but also changes the hash reference that points to the updated transaction. The updated hash reference (R2) is valid as it correctly points to the new transaction data. However, the updated hash reference is part of a Merkle tree whose root is a hash reference as well. The root of the Merkle tree (R12) points to a piece of data that contains the hash references R1 and R2. The latter one has been changed in order to be consistent with the manipulated version of Transaction 2. Hence, the cryptographic hash value of the piece of data containing the updated version of R2 changes as well, which in turn invalidates the root of the Merkle tree R12.

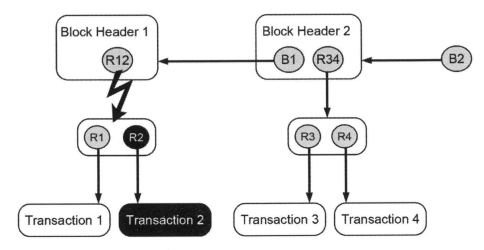

Figure 15-6. Changing a transaction and its hash reference in the Merkle tree invalidates the root of the Merkle tree, which invalidates the whole data structure

Replacing a Transaction

Figure 15-7 considers the case of replacing a whole transaction instead of only manipulating details of an existing transaction and updating its hash reference.

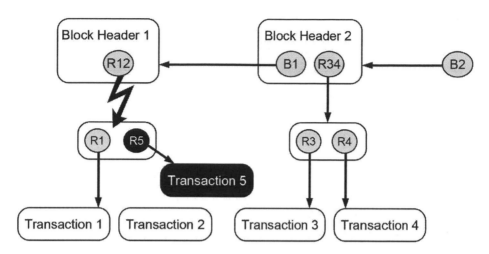

Figure 15-7. Replacing a transaction and its hash reference in the Merkle tree invalidates the root of the Merkle tree, which invalidates the whole data structure

When you compare Figure 15-6 with Figure 15-7, you can only find minor difference regarding the name of the transaction and its hash reference. Concerning the consequences, both illustrations are identical. In both cases the root of the Merkle tree R12 will be invalid due to changes that happened within the Merkle tree. As a result, we find that changing a transaction or replacing a transaction will have the same impact on the blockchain-data-structure. The manipulation will be detected in both cases and will invalidate the whole data structure.

■ **Note**　Changing or replacing data in the blockchain-data-structure will have identical results as both have identical effects on hash references.

Changing the Merkle Root

Figure 15-8 illustrates what happens if a whole Merkle tree, including its root, is changed.

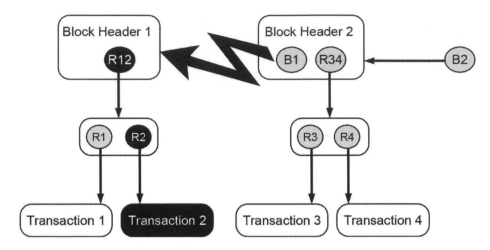

Figure 15-8. Changing a Merkle tree invalidates the hash reference that points to the block header that contains it, which in turn invalidates the whole data structure

The root of the manipulated Merkle tree (R12) is part of a block header (Block Header 1). The change of the Merkle root changes the cryptographic hash value of Block Header 1, which in turn causes the hash reference that points to it (B1) to be invalid. The hash reference B1 that maintains the connection or serves as a link from Block Header 2 to Block Header 1 becomes invalid as it detects the change. As a result, the whole blockchain-data-structure becomes invalid.

Changing a Block Header Reference

Figure 15-9 illustrates what happens if not only a whole Merkle tree but also the hash reference to the manipulated block header is changed.

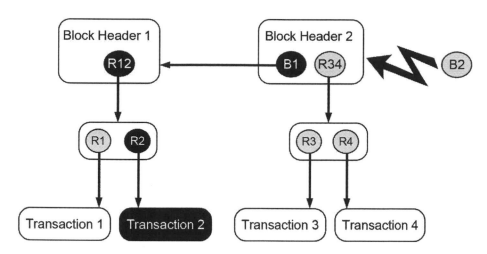

Figure 15-9. Changing a hash reference within a block header invalidates the hash reference that points to the manipulated block header, which in turn invalidates the whole data structure

If the hash reference (B1) to the manipulated block header (Block Header 1) is changed, the following happens: Starting with hash reference B1, all hash references that point toward the manipulated data are consistent and valid since they were adjusted to the performed manipulation. However, the manipulated hash reference B1 is part of Block Header 2 and hence its cryptographic hash value changes, which in turn invalidates the hash reference B2 that pointed to the original data block header containing the original version of the hash reference B1. As a result, the whole blockchain-data-structure is invalid as well.

Changing Data Orderly

After this discussion of the many approaches to manipulate the blockchain-data-structure, which all yielded an invalid data structure, it is time to illustrate what needs to be done to change or update the blockchain-data-structure orderly. Figure 15-10 illustrates how to change the blockchain-data-structure in the correct way.

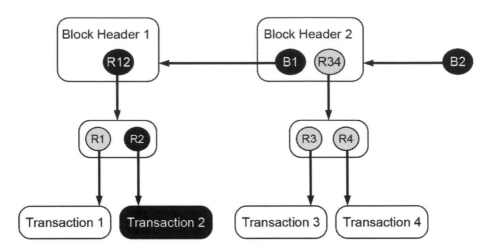

Figure 15-10. Changing a transaction orderly includes changing all subsequent hash references

If we consider changing or updating some details of Transaction 2, we have to subsequently update the whole sequence of hash references: R2, R12, B1, and B2. This means that all hash references, starting with the one that directly points to the manipulated data and ending with the hash reference that points to the most recent block header as well as all hash references in between them, need to be changed and updated so that they reflect the changes of their targets. This is quite an elaborate task. And it is an elaborate process on purpose. All of this work is necessary to keep the whole blockchain-data-structure consistent and to keep its integrity. All other attempts to change or manipulate data that are part of the blockchain-data-structure will cause invalid hash references, which in turn will invalidate the whole data structure.

Intended vs. Unintended Changes

The preceding discussion showed that the blockchain-data-structure pursues a radical all-or-nothing approach when it comes to changing its data: One either changes the whole data structure completely from the point that causes the change until the head of the whole chain or one better leave it all unchanged in the first place. All other half-hearted, halfway through, or partial changes will leave the whole blockchain-data-structure in an inconsistent state, which will be detected easily and quickly. This is due to the properties of hash references, where the blockchain-data-structure does not differentiate between intended or unintended changes. Actually there are no such things as intended or unintended changes in the blockchain. These words refer to a valuation of the motives or the person who caused a change. But the blockchain-data-structure values neither the motives nor the person who causes an inconsistency. The blockchain only cares about correctness and consistency of all its hash references. If one of them is invalid, the whole data structure is invalid, regardless of who or what caused that change or why it was made. And this property makes the blockchain-data-structure very valuable.

Outlook

This step illustrated in great detail how the blockchain-data-structure deals with changes of its data. It turned out that the blockchain-data-structure is very change sensitive. It pursues a radical all-or-nothing approach when it comes to changing its data. The next step explains how this property can be used to make data unchangeable, which makes the blockchain-data-structure the perfect candidate for storing data in an unreliable and untrustworthy environment.

Summary

- The steps to be performed in order to add new transaction data to the blockchain-data-structure are:
  - Create a new Merkle tree that contains all new transaction data to be added.
  - Create a new block header that contains both a hash reference to its preceding header and the root of the Merkle tree that contains the new transaction data.
  - Create a hash reference to the new block header, which is now the current head of the blockchain-data-structure.

- Changing data in the blockchain-data-structure requires renewing all hash references starting with the one that directly points to the manipulated data and ending with the head of the whole blockchain-data-structure as well as all hash references in between them.

- The blockchain-data-structure pursues a radical all-or-nothing approach when it comes to changing its data: One either changes the whole data structure completely starting from the point that causes the change until the head of the whole chain or one better leave it unchanged in the first place.

- All half-hearted, halfway through, or partial changes will leave the whole blockchain-data-structure in an inconsistent state, which will be detected easily and quickly.

- Changing the blockchain-data-structure completely is a very elaborate process on purpose.

- The high sensitivity of the blockchain-data-structure regarding changes is due to the properties of hash references.

Protecting the Data Store

Discovering the power of immutability

Step 15 concluded with the finding that the blockchain-data-structure stores data in a change-sensitive manner. Any alteration of data stored in the block-chain-data-structure will stand out and require an elaborate process for incorporating it into the existing structure. This step explains how that property can be used to prepare the history of transaction data to be shared and distributed in an untrustworthy environment without having to fear that dishonest members of a peer-to-peer system can manipulate its content for its own advantage.

The Metaphor

Let's assume I want to pretend to be a member of a prestigious aristocratic family. How could I achieve that? Forging my family tree could do that. For example, I could make up an aristocratic grandfather and connect myself to him with a forged family tree. Will this suffice to convince others from my fake aristocratic roots? Well, this fake will be quickly uncovered since family trees rarely exist in isolation; instead, they are connected and interwoven with other family trees via family relationships. Hence, if none of the family trees

© Daniel Drescher 2017

D. Drescher, *Blockchain Basics*, DOI 10.1007/978-1-4842-2604-9_16

of the established aristocratic families have a reference or relation to my fictional grandfather, my fictional family history will be quickly discovered as fake. In order to get my fictional family accepted, I would need to forge the family documents of some of the established aristocratic families by embedding references to my fictional family tree in their family history. But even this may not suffice. Real people have real lives and leave their footprints in our world. But my fictional grandfather never really lived. Hence, I have to make up his life in order to make the fake appear real. This implies that I have to invent the entire life of my fictional grandfather, including his childhood as well as his education and career history. Additionally, the supporting documents would also need to be faked, such as the birth certificate, school registration documents, school certificates, university degrees, professional certifications, memberships, and so on. Schools, universities, and employers maintain records of their students and employees and publish almanacs and photographs of social events. Hence, it would be necessary to manipulate their documents as well in order to make my fictional grandfather a former member of these institutions. Since manipulating all these documents would be complicated and costly, I probably would decide to stay with my real but nonaristocratic family history.

This intellectual game illustrates that forging the past is possible but extremely expensive, since it requires rewriting and forging large parts of history in order to embed the fake information into many documents and references of the true history. The costs of doing so are prohibitively high; hence, it is much easier and less expensive to stick with the truth. This step explains how the blockchain utilizes this finding in order to protect its history of transaction data from being forged.

The Goal

It is important that the whole history of transaction data maintained by the blockchain always represents the truth and therefore makes it a trustworthy source for clarifying ownership-related matters.

The Challenge

The blockchain is a purely distributed peer-to-peer system that is open to everyone. Hence, there is a risk that dishonest peers could manipulate or forge the history of transaction data for their own advantage. The challenge is to keep the system open to everyone yet protect the history of transaction data from being forged or manipulated.

The Idea

Distinguishing honest from dishonest nodes in an open system in advance is hard or even impossible. Hence, in order to protect the history of transactions from being manipulated by dishonest nodes, we want to prevent anyone from manipulating the history in the first place. If no one can change the history of transaction data, regardless of whether it is honest or dishonest, we do not have to fear that it can be manipulated at all. Hence, making the history of transaction data unchangeable in the first place solves the problem. As a result, the system can stay open to everyone and no one has to worry about dishonest nodes manipulating the history of transactions.

A Short Detour to Immutability

Immutability means that something cannot be changed. Data that are immutable cannot be changed once they have been created or written. For that reason, these data are also called read-only data. Their whole benefit is solely presenting information for reading or presentation purposes. This fact is particularly desirable if one needs to give data to others and hence loses control on how the data are used. Handing over immutable data is an effective way of preventing changes or manipulation of data. Driver's licenses, passports, and educational certificates are examples of immutable objects in real life. Authorities produce them in order to document something and their only legible use is to be shown and to be read.

How It Works: The Big Picture

The main idea used by the blockchain to make the transaction history immutable is to make changing it prohibitively costly and make those costs deter everyone from changing it. Making the history of transaction data immutable has three elements:

1. Storing the history of transaction data in a way that even the smallest manipulation of its content stands out and becomes noticeable.

2. Enforcing that embedding a manipulation in the transaction history requires rewriting a huge part of it.

3. Making adding, writing, or rewriting of data to the history computationally expensive.

Making Manipulations Stand Out

The blockchain-data-structure that stores data in a change-sensitive manner fulfills the first element. As a result, one cannot silently manipulate data that are part of the blockchain-data-structure and hope that no one will notice it. Any change will stand out with a huge "noise" caused by breaking hash references that become invalid as a result of changing the data they refer to.

Enforcing Rewriting the History for Embedding Changes

The blockchain-data-structure also fulfills the second element because it pursues a radical all-or-nothing approach when it comes to changing its data: One either changes the data structure starting from the point that causes the change until the head of the whole chain or one better leave it unchanged in the first place.

Making Adding Data Computationally Expensive

The third element is for those who are not afraid to rewrite large parts of the blockchain-data-structure in the course of having a manipulation embedded in the transaction history. But as soon as writing or rewriting the blockchain-data-structure incurs huge computational costs, people will think twice about whether changing it was a good idea in the first place.

The blockchain-technology-suite makes the content of the blockchain-data-structure immutable by incurring significant computational costs for every block being written, rewritten, or added to the blockchain-data-structure. The computational costs are incurred by hash puzzles that are unique for each block header.[1] As a result, one either accepts the whole cost of changing the data structure from the point that causes the change until the head of the chain by solving a hash puzzle for every block header involved or it is better to leave it unchanged.

---

[1] Nakamoto, Satoshi. Bitcoin: A peer-to-peer electronic cash system. 2008. https://bitcoin.org/bitcoin.pdf.

How It Works: The Details

The procedure to add a new block to the blockchain-data-structure, as discussed in Step 15, is not computationally expensive because it only requires adding the hash reference that points to the current head of the chain to the new block header and declaring it as the new head of the chain. The challenge of making the blockchain-data-structure immutable is to make adding a new block a computationally expensive task. The following aspects need to be considered in the course of achieving this:

- Compulsory data of block headers
- The process of creating a new block header
- Validation rules for block headers

Compulsory Data

Every block header of the blockchain-data-structure has to carry at least the following data[2]:

- The root of a Merkle tree containing transaction data
- A hash reference to the header of the preceding block
- The difficulty level of the hash puzzle
- The time when solving the hash puzzle started
- The nonce that solves the hash puzzle

The Process of Creating A New Block

Creating a new block involves the following steps:

1. Get the root of the Merkle tree that contains the transaction data to be added.

2. Create a hash reference to the header of that block that will be the predecessor from the new block header's point of view.

3. Obtain the required difficulty level.

---

[2]Okupski, Krzysztof. Bitcoin developer reference. Working paper. 2014.

4. Get the current time.

5. Create a preliminary block header that contains the data mentioned in points 1 to 4.

6. Solve the hash puzzle for the preliminary block header.

7. Finish the new block by adding the nonce that solves the hash puzzle to the preliminary header.

Figure 16-1 illustrates the hash puzzle that needs to be solved when adding a new block to the blockchain-data-structure. It shows the data of the block header whose hash value has to fulfill the given restriction or difficulty level, respectively. Note that the difficulty level is part of the block header and hence is also part of the block's hash value. This ensures that no one can bypass the computational costs of the hash puzzle by arbitrarily reducing the difficulty level.

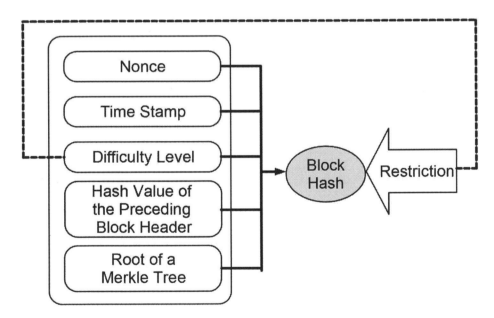

Figure 16-1. Schematic illustration of the hash puzzle required to be solved when adding a new block to the blockchain-data-structure

Validation Rules

Every block header of has to fulfill the following rules:

1. It must contain a valid hash reference to a previous block.

2. It must contain a valid root of a Merkle tree containing transaction data.

3. It must contain a correct difficulty level.

4. Its time stamp is after the time stamp of its preceding block header.

5. It must contain a nonce.

6. The hash value of all the five pieces of data combined together fulfills the difficulty level.

The validation rules ensure that only those blocks are added to the blockchain-data-structure for which the hash puzzle was solved and the computational costs were paid. Rule 4 ensures that the blocks and the transaction data are indeed ordered according to the time being added.

▓ **Note**   The activity of adding a new block to the blockchain-data-structure by solving a hash puzzle is also called mining or block mining.

Why It Works

The blockchain-data-structure makes any change of its data stand out due to the fragility of the hash references with respect to changes of the data being referred. This causes the need to rewrite all blocks that are affected by a manipulation. The hash puzzle causes costs for every block that needs to be rewritten in the course of embedding a manipulation. The accumulated costs of rewriting the blockchain-data-structure in the course of embedding a manipulation make it unattractive to manipulate the transaction history in the first place. As a result, the blockchain-data-structure becomes an immutable append-only data store.

The Costs of Manipulating the Blockchain-Data-Structure

Let's assume we were going to try to manipulate a particular piece of transaction data that is part of a Merkle tree whose root belongs to a block header located 20 blocks below the current head of the blockchain-data-structure. Embedding the manipulated transaction data requires the following work:

1. Rewrite the Merkle tree to which the manipulated transaction belongs.

2. Rewrite the block header to which the root of the rewritten Merkle tree belongs.

3. Rewrite all succeeding block headers up to the head of the blockchain-data-structure.

Point 2 requires the solution of a hash puzzle because changing the Merkle root changes the hash value of the block header and hence the solution of its hash puzzle. Point 3 requires solving 20 hash puzzles due to successive changes of the hash references to the previous block header. Under the assumption that solving a hash puzzle takes on average 10 minutes, we would need in total 210 minutes to embed a manipulation in a transaction that belongs to a block header located 20 blocks below the current head. These huge costs deter nodes from changing the blockchain-data-structure.

The Immutable Data Store in the Real World

The immutability of the blockchain-data-structure depends on the computational costs induced by the hash puzzle. The difficulty of the hash puzzles determines how much computational effort and hence how much time is needed to solve them, which in turn determines the immutability of the blockchain-data-structure. If the difficulty is too low, the computational costs of changing the blockchain-data-structure will decline and may no longer be regarded as prohibitively high, which in turn may encourage nodes to manipulate the history of transaction data. On the other hand, if the difficulty is too high, even the computational costs of adding a new block may be regarded as prohibitively high, which in turn discourages nodes from adding new transaction data. Hence, a challenge in designing a blockchain is to determine the appropriate level of difficulty for the hash puzzles. This challenge is even more demanding as computational power of computers changes due to technical advances. As a result, the difficulty level may need to be determined dynamically.

Blockchain applications in the real world rarely utilize a constant difficulty level for all blocks. Instead they typically utilize a dynamic difficulty level based on the speed at which new blocks are added.[3] This ensures that the time needed to solve the hash puzzle stays at a level that prevents nodes from manipulating the history of transaction data while the actual computational effort may increase.

---

[3]Okupski, Krzysztof. Bitcoin developer reference. Working paper. 2014; Wood, Gavin. Ethereum: A secure decentralized generalized transaction ledger. 2014. http://gavwood.com/paper.pdf.

Outlook

This step explained that the blockchain prevents the history of transaction data from being manipulated or forged by turning the blockchain-data-structure into an immutable append-only data store. The next step focuses on making that data store available to everyone in a distributed peer-to-peer system.

Summary

- The blockchain protects the history of transaction data from manipulation and forgery by storing transaction data in an immutable data store.

- The history of a transaction is made immutable by utilizing two ideas:

    - Storing the transaction data in the change-sensitive blockchain-data-structure, which when being changed requires rewriting the data structure starting at the point that causes the change until the head of the whole chain.

    - Requiring the solution of a hash puzzle for writing, rewriting, or adding every single block header in the blockchain-data-structure.

- The hash puzzle is unique for each block header because it depends on its unique content.

- The need to rewrite the blockchain-data-structure when it is changed and the costs of doing so make it unattractive to manipulate the history of transaction data in the first place.

- Requiring the solution of a hash puzzle for every writing, rewriting or adding of block headers in the blockchain-data-structure turns is into an append-only data store.

- A block header contains at least the following data:

    - A hash reference to the header of its preceding block

    - The root of a Merkle tree that contains transaction data

    - The difficulty of its hash puzzle

    - The time when solving the hash puzzle was started

    - The nonce that solves the hash puzzle

Distributing the Data Store Among Peers

When computers gossip

Step 16 turned the blockchain-data-structure into an immutable append-only data store, which can be used as a manipulation-resistant ledger for transaction data. Having one immutable append-only history of transaction data in insolation may be of limited value for the goal of clarifying ownership based on a group of computers that acts as witnesses of ownership-related events. Hence, this step focuses on establishing a purely distributed peer-to-peer system that allows sharing of information about transactions.

The Metaphor

What is the best way to spread some personal news among all employees of a company if you do not have access to a global e-mail distribution list? One approach that guarantees that all employees will eventually receive the news is to share it with one or two well-connected and chatty colleagues and ask

© Daniel Drescher 2017
D. Drescher, *Blockchain Basics*, DOI 10.1007/978-1-4842-2604-9_17

them to keep the news a secret. This approach works out because there is almost no other information that is more quickly exchanged among colleagues than personal news that is shared under conditions of confidentiality. The reason for this fact is quite simple: Human beings are social creatures who have a genuine interest in their peers, and sharing information about others is a usual behavioral pattern for renewing or strengthening social connections. This step considers an aspect of the blockchain that may portray peer-to-peer systems in a different and almost human light. The aspect that is discussed in this step is the exchange of information among computers by means of communication.

The Goal

The blockchain is a purely distributed peer-to-peer system for managing ownership. It consists of individual computers that maintain their own version of an immutable ledger that stores the whole history of transaction data. Hence, the individual computers are equivalent to witnesses who can testify whether a certain transaction has happened according to their own memories. But how do the individual computers observe or learn about transactions in the first place? Hence, the major goal of this step is to ensure that the individual computers that make up the peer-to-peer system get informed about transactions and are able to maintain their own history of transaction data.

The Challenge

A purely distributed peer-to-peer system does not have any central point of coordination or control. Hence, there is no central component that spreads information to all computers that make up the system. The existence of such a central information point would be a contradiction in terms. In addition, the distribution of information can fail due to technical problems. Hence, the challenge is to have all nodes of the system receiving information of all transactions without falling back to a central component.

The Idea

The idea is to let the computers that make up the peer-to-peer system share and exchange information in the same fashion as humans share news. If the nodes of the peer-to-peer system forward information to their peer nodes, which in turn forward the information to their peers, then eventually all nodes in the system will receive the information.

On a more detailed level, the peer-to-peer system will mimic the way in which groups of humans, such as employees of a company, groups of friends, or the members of a sports club, communicate with one another. In a nutshell, the members of these groups are engaged in three different kinds of conversations that serve district purposes:

- Small talk, which serves an important purpose from a social point of view as it keeps existing relationships alive but it does not contain any substantial information.

- News, comprising conversations in which substantial information is exchanged among the participants.

- Introducing new peers, the kinds of conversations that are necessary to let new people join the existing group of friends or colleagues. Establishing a new relationship and accepting a new member to a group always require some form of initiation rite. This is the point where aspiring members are made familiar with the group's history and their values and are introduced to prominent members of the group.

How It Works: The Overview[1]

Peer-to-peer systems of computers are the digital equivalent to groups of people. The individual computers that make up the peer-to-peer system also have small talk, exchange news, and accept new members through an initiation rite. These interactions are an integral part of any peer-to-peer system. Similar to human beings who communicate with one another via the medium of spoken words, computers in a distributed peer-to-peer system communicate via a digital network. The largest network that connects a huge number of computers is the Internet. Hence, the least expensive way to construct a peer-to-peer system is to let the nodes communicate with one another over the Internet. Hence, the distributed peer-to-peer system utilizing the Internet as a medium of communication is characterized by the following facts:

- Each computer is connected with the system through the Internet.

- Each computer is identified by a unique address.

- Each computer can disconnect and reconnect with the system at any given time.

- Each computer independently maintains a list of peers it communicates with.

- Communication between nodes is based on messages.

- Messages are sent from one node to another over the Internet by using their unique Internet addresses.

---

[1]Tanenbaum, Andrew S., and Maarten Van Steen. *Distributed systems: principles and paradigms* (2nd ed.). Upper Saddle River, NJ: Pearson Prentice Hall, 2007; Tanenbaum, Andrew S., and David J. Wetherall. *Computer networks* (5th ed.). Upper Saddle River, NJ: Prentice Hall, 2010.

The fact that the nodes communicate over a network and that they can disconnect and reconnect at any time influences the delivery of messages. The delivery of messages in such a network has the following characteristics:

- Messages are not guaranteed to arrive at the addressees, they may get lost instead.

- Messages may arrive more than once.

- Messages may arrive in a different order than they were sent.

These characteristics cause some hurdles in the communication, but they are solved in the following ways:

- Messages are sent in a gossip style. Every node that receives new information will forward it to the peers it communicates with, which in turn will handle the news in the same way. This ensures that eventually every node receives the news, even if some individual messages get lost.

- Due to the fact that messages can be identified by their digital fingerprint or cryptographic hash value, nodes can identify duplicates easily and ignore them.

- The fact that transaction data as well as block headers contain time stamps allows the nodes to order them based on an objective criterion.

How It Works: The Details

The communication between the nodes that make up the distributed peer-to-peer system has the following three purposes:

- Keeping existing connections alive

- Establishing new connections

- Distributing new information

The first two kinds of communication are mainly focused on the peer-to-peer system itself. They are concerned with keeping the network of peers together and doing some digital housekeeping. But the purpose of the peer-to-peer system is not keeping itself busy just for the sake of staying busy. Instead, the purpose of the peer-to-peer system is the management of ownership. Hence, the third type of communication focuses on new transaction data and new blocks to be added to the blockchain-data-structure. This information is needed by every node of the system in order to maintain its own version of the transaction history.

Keeping Existing Connections Alive

Each computer in the network independently maintains a list of peers it communicates with. This list contains only a subset of all nodes that make up the whole system. This is similar to employees who maintain social connections to some of their colleagues, comprising only a subgroup of all the employees of the same company. On a regular basis, each computer verifies that these peers are still available. This is done by sending peers a small message, often called ping, with the request to answer it with a message called pong. Peers that repeatedly do not answer these messages are removed from the list of peers. This is similar to small talk between colleagues, which mainly serves the purpose of keeping the social relationship alive.

Establishing New Connections

Every computer can request to join the peer-to-peer system by sending a corresponding request message to any of the nodes that make up the system. The requested node adds the address of the inquirer to its list of peers and sends a confirmation as reply. When receiving the reply the node will add the address of the sender to its own list of peers as well. As a result, a new connection is established and the system has grown by one more node. Having only one connection to the system is risky as every node can terminate a connection, shut down, or even crash at any time. Hence, when joining a peer-to-peer system, a computer typically establishes connections to many different nodes that are already part of the system. This ensures that the connection to the system as a whole is maintained, even if individual nodes disconnect or shut down.

Distributing New Information

This kind of communication serves the application goal of the system that is managing ownership. This is done by forwarding new transaction data and new blocks to be added to the blockchain-data-structure in a gossip type of information forwarding. Sharing ownership-related information happens in the following three occasions:

- In an ongoing fashion: new information (e.g., new transaction data and new blocks) are distributed as they occur. Every node connected to the system will eventually receive all news.

- As an update: nodes that reconnect to the system after they were disconnected for a while will receive all transaction data and blocks they have missed out in the meantime.

- As part of the on-boarding procedure: new nodes that join the system have not had the chance to build their own history of transactions because they have never been connected with the system before. Hence, they need to get the whole history of transactions that happened up to the time they joined the system. Transferring a copy of the whole up-to-date version of the blockchain-data-structure to the newbie node ensures that it becomes a full-fledged node after joining the system. This type of information delivery can be seen as an extreme case of an update: an update of the whole history of transactions that have ever happened in the system.

Why It Works

The different kinds of communication ensure that new computers can join the system and hence contribute to its growth. Additionally, the system is kept together based on communication that focuses on establishing new and maintaining existing connections. Most important, the system utilizes a gossip type of communication that ensures that eventually all members of the peer-to-peer system will receive all transaction data and blocks to be added to the blockchain-data-structure.

Outlook

This step focused on how individual computers become nodes of a distributed peer-to-peer system and how the computers that make up the system communicate with one another. In particular, this step focused on the aspects of message delivery in an unreliable network. However, this discussion did not consider what the individual nodes do with the information once they received it, but processing information is as important as receiving information. Hence, the next step discusses how transaction data are processed within the individual nodes.

Summary

- Computers in a distributed peer-to-peer system communicate with one another via a digital network.

- Due to the omnipresence of the Internet, it is compelling to create a distributed peer-to-peer system by connecting the individual nodes via the Internet.

- A peer-to-peer system that uses the Internet as a medium of communication is characterized by the following facts:

  - The computers are connected with one another via the Internet.

  - Each computer is identified by a unique address.

  - Each computer can disconnect and reconnect to the system at any given time.

  - Each computer independently maintains a list of peers with which it communicates.

  - Communication between nodes is based on messages.

  - Messages are sent from one node to another over the Internet by using their unique addresses.

- Due to the adversaries of networks, the communication among the nodes is characterized by the following facts:

  - Messages are not guaranteed to arrive at the addressees, but they may get lost instead.

  - Messages may arrive more than once.

  - Messages may arrive in a different order than they were sent.

- The blockchain counteracts the adversaries of communicating over an unreliable network in the following ways:

  - Messages are sent in a gossip style. Every node that receives a message will forward it to the peers it communicates with, which in turn will handle the message in the same way.

  - Duplicates of transactions or blocks are identified and filtered out based on their cryptographic hash values.

  - Each node can order the received information because transaction data and block headers contain time stamps.

- The communication among the computers that make up the peer-to-peer system serves the following three purposes:

  - Keeping existing connections alive

  - Establishing new connections

  - Distributing new information

- Forwarding ownership-related information happens on three occasions:

  - In an ongoing fashion by forwarding new transaction data and new blocks to all nodes that are connected to the system

  - As an update for nodes that reconnect to the system after being disconnected for a while

  - As part of the on-boarding procedure that transfers a copy of the whole up-to-date version of the blockchain-data-structure to the new nodes to ensure that they become full-fledged nodes after joining the system

Verifying and Adding Transactions

Ruling a group of computers with carrot and stick

In Step 17 individual computers were turned into nodes of a purely distributed peer-to-peer system that communicate with one another about transaction data and new blocks to be added to the blockchain-data-structure. This step focuses on what happens once a node receives transaction data and how to ensure that only valid transaction data and blocks are added to the blockchain-data-structure.

The Metaphor

Let's consider a company that offers a simple service: grading multiple-choice tests for schools and universities. Schools and universities can send the multiple-choice answer forms of their students together with the correct

© Daniel Drescher 2017
D. Drescher, *Blockchain Basics*, DOI 10.1007/978-1-4842-2604-9_18

solutions to the company, which in turn will grade all of the answer sheets. Unfortunately, the employees of the company show little motivation to do their job well. As a result, the company turns all of its employees into contractors who only receive a performance-related compensation that is governed by the following three rules:

1. All answer sheets to be marked, the solutions as well as all marked answer sheets are available to all contractors at any time through the company's software system.

2. Only the first contractor who marks an answer sheet correctly receives one dollar as a reward.

3. If a contractor finds out that another contractor marked an answer sheet incorrectly, the contractor who made the mistake has to repay the compensation and the one who found and corrected the mistake will receive the compensation instead.

Consequences

There are several consequences for the rules of the above scenario:

*   Due to the fact that the contractors only receive performance-related compensation, they have a strong economic incentive to follow the rules.

*   Due to rule 1, all contractors have the same chance to contribute work and earn money.

*   Due to rule 1, all contractors have the necessary information to control and correct the work of their coworkers.

*   Due to rule 2, each contractor has an incentive to work fast. However, the quality of work may suffer due to speed.

*   Due to rule 3, each contractor has an incentive to work conscientiously.

*   Due to rule 3, each contractor has an incentive to control and correct the work of its coworkers.

Due to these rules, the efficiency of the company increased significantly but after some months, the company received massive complaints from its customers. The quality of work had dropped dramatically. It seems that all multiple-choice tests were marked completely randomly. After doing some research, the company found that the contractors had made a pact. They agreed among themselves not to control any coworker's results and instead to do the marking as quickly as possible. Since assigning marks randomly is the fastest way to do the job, all contractors eventually ended up using that marking strategy.

The lesson learned from this metaphor is that the combination of reward, punishment, peer pressure, and competition can be used to manage a group of independently acting individuals as long as they do not collectively counteract.

This step explains the blockchain-algorithm, which it is nothing more than a clever implementation of the carrot-and-stick approach combined with competition and peer pressure that works in a similar fashion as the company in this example. However, the challenge is to get all the details right.

The Goal

The goal is to allow everyone to add new transaction data to the history of transaction data while preserving its integrity.

The Challenge

The blockchain is completely open. Everyone, even the most dishonest, can connect computers to the system and as a result can create transactions and send them to all other nodes that make up the system. As a result, it cannot be guaranteed that the transactions sent through the network are correct. Hence, the challenge is to keep the system open to everyone while ensuring that only valid transactions are added.

The Idea

In order to ensure that only valid transactions are added to the system, all nodes of the system are allowed to also act as supervisors of their peers and reward them for adding valid and authorized transactions and for finding errors in the work of others. As a result, all nodes of the system have an incentive to process transactions correctly and to supervise and point out any mistake made by any of its peers.[1]

How It Works: The Building Blocks

The blockchain-algorithm is a sequence of instructions that governs how nodes process new transaction data and blocks. The individual rules and procedures can be traced back to the following building blocks:

- Validation rules
- Reward

[1]Nakamoto, Satoshi. Bitcoin: A peer-to-peer electronic cash system. 2008. https:// bitcoin.org/bitcoin.pdf.

- Punishment
- Competition
- Peer control

Validation Rules

The ultimate goal of the blockchain-algorithm is to ensure that the block-chain-data-structure only contains valid blocks, which in turn consist of valid transaction data and valid block headers. The validity of these data is evaluated based on two distinct groups of validation rules:

- Validation rules for transaction data
- Validation rules for block headers

Validation Rules for Transaction Data

Validation rules for transaction data define which data are required for describing a transaction. These rules encompass formal correctness, semantic correctness, and authorization. Step 9 discussed the validation rules for transaction data. These rules are specific to the application goal of the blockchain. Hence, a blockchain for managing ownership in digital bonus points may have different validation rules than a blockchain that manages ownership of real estate.

Validation Rules for Block Headers

The validation rules for block headers focus on the formal and semantic correctness of the block headers. These rules are agnostic to the content of the transaction data; instead they are concerned with the way information is added to the blockchain-data-structure. Step 16 discussed the compulsory data of block headers and their validation rules. A central element of validating block headers is the verification of the proof of work or the has puzzle respectively. Only blocks whose headers contains a correct solution of its individual hash puzzle are processed further. Every block whose header fails the verification of its proof of work is discarded immediately.

Reward

Creating valid blocks costs energy, time, and money because it requires solving the computationally expensive hash puzzle that is unique for every block. The hash puzzle is the integral element to make the blockchain-data-structure immutable. Hence, solving the hash puzzle is absolutely indispensible and so are the entailed costs. The only way to convince peers to carry the burden of solving the hash puzzle is to offer them a reward as compensation for their work. Hence, the blockchain-algorithm defines how nodes that submit valid blocks are rewarded. From a more abstract point of view, one can state that the reward is the compensation for all burdens related to achieve and maintain the integrity of the whole system.

Punishment

Reward is only one instrument to provide peers an incentive to validate transaction data and to create valid blocks. The blockchain also needs a way to punish peers for counteracting the integrity of the system. Typical measures of punishment are reclaiming the reward for blocks that were accepted in the past but were identified as invalid or useless later on. Another form of punishment is the absence of reward. Letting nodes do the proof of work but not rewarding them because of identifying the block as duplicate, being too old, or being useless is a punishment in its own right. This is true since the creation of a valid block requires the solution of an hash puzzle, which in turn incurs costs. Not getting rewarded for creating a block implies that the costs for creating it cannot be covered. Hence, not realizing a reward is a form of punishment too.

Competition

Rewarding nodes for submitting valid blocks is a core concept of the blockchain-algorithm, but handing out rewards costs resources. Hence, it is important to prevent wasting resources by giving rewards to nodes that do not contribute significantly to the maintenance of the system. The best way to achieve a high quality of work while reducing costs is to establish a competition for rewards based on a well-defined criterion. The blockchain-algorithm holds a continuous competition for rewards based on two criteria. The competition is actually a combination of the following competitions that are held sequentially:

- Speed competition
- Quality competition

Only the node that wins both competitions receives the reward for submitting a new block. The trick of the competition is that the losers of the speed competition are the referees in the quality competition, and they validate the block that the winner of the speed competition submits. This ensures a strict examination of the submitted block.

Speed Competition

The speed competition among the nodes is based on the hash puzzle. The central element of creating a valid block is creating the proof of work, which means solving the unique hash puzzle of the new block. Based on the nature of cryptographic hash functions, solving the hash puzzle takes an unknown period of time. There is no way to solve a hash puzzle in advance because the puzzle depends on the content of the block itself. As a result, all nodes take part in a competition for solving the hash puzzle of a new block. Once a node submits a new block, the speed competition is over. The first node that submits a new block with a valid solution of its hash puzzle is the winner of the speed competition and becomes the only candidate in the quality competition.

Quality Competition

The quality competition focuses on the correctness of the submitted block. Once a node submits a new block, it is sent to all nodes of the system. By receiving a new block, each node has to act as a referee in the quality competition, which means validating the new block based on the validation rules for transaction data and block headers. If the block is found valid, the node that submitted the new block receives the reward and a new speed competition opens with transaction data that were left over or have arrived in the meantime. If the block is found to be invalid, it is thrown away and the speed competition reopens with all the transactions that were already at stake.

The quality competition has an interesting aspect of peer control. By receiving a new block, each node realizes that it has already lost the speed competition and that it has to work as a referee in the quality competition. It goes without saying that these referees are the most meticulous and strict referees one can imagine because they have already lost the speed competition and hence have nothing more to lose. Actually, all nodes know that they can get back in the game for the reward if they can prove that the submitted block is invalid. In this case, the speed competition reopens and they have the chance to finish their own block, whose completion was interrupted, and to win the race themselves. As a result, the quality competition or the examination of the submitted block, respectively, will be done at a very high level of accuracy.

Peer Control

Even the best rules are useless if no one follows them, observes that they were followed, and enforces their fulfillment. Unfortunately, purely distributed peer-to-peer systems neither have nor would accept a central point of control or coordination that could supervise the adherence to the rules and enforce their implementation. Hence, the blockchain-algorithm makes all nodes of the system the supervisors of all other nodes. The nodes of the system are work-

ers and supervisors at the same time because they verify transactions and
create new blocks while receiving, reviewing, and validating the blocks created
by other nodes as well. The work of each node contributes to the creation
of new valid blocks as well as to the detection, refusal, or removal of invalid
transaction data or invalid blocks.

How It Works: The Skeleton

The rules of the competition establish a simple two-step rhythm that governs
the work of every node in the network. At any given point in time, all nodes
of the system are in either of the two phases:

1. Evaluating a new block that was created and submitted by
    one of the peers

2. Trying hard to be the next node that creates a new block
    that in turn has to be evaluated by all others

One of the most important results of the blockchain-algorithm is that it not
only ensures validation of transaction data and blocks but also ensures all
nodes have an identical working rhythm. This identical working rhythm is the
core concept to ensure that all blocks maintain an identical history of transaction data. However, the working rhythm is not imposed on the nodes by a
central clock because that would be a contradiction to the purely distributed
nature of the system. What makes the rhythm tick is the arrival of messages
at the individual nodes. As soon as a node receives a message that contains a
new block, it switches to the evaluation phase; and as soon as the evaluation
phase finishes, the node switches back to verifying new transaction data and
creating a new block itself.

How It Works: The Details

The procedure that governs how nodes deal with new transaction data and
blocks they receive from their peers consists of the following rules (the rules
printed in bold are the one that establish the two-step rhythm):

1. New transaction data as well as new blocks are for-
    warded to all nodes in a gossip fashion.

2. Each node collects new transaction data in an inbox and
    selects them for processing.

3. **Each node processes new blocks immediately with highest priority.**

4. Each node processes new transaction data by validating them for authorization and formal and semantic correctness.

5. Each node collects only valid transaction data into a Merkle tree and starts creating a new block by solving its hash puzzle.

6. **As soon as a node finishes the hash puzzle, it sends the newly created block to all other nodes.**

7. Each node processes new blocks by verifying the solution of its hash puzzle and by verifying all its containing transaction data for formal correctness, semantic correctness, and authorization.

8. Each node adds valid blocks to its own copy of the blockchain-data-structure.

9. If a newly arrived block has been identified as invalid, it will be discarded and the nodes continue with processing transaction data or with finishing the hash puzzle of a new block.

10. If a newly arrived block has been identified as valid, the node removes those transactions that are contained in the new block from its own inbox and starts with processing transaction data and the creation of a new block.

11. If a block that was added to the blockchain-data-structure is identified as invalid or useless later on, that block as well as all its subsequent blocks will be removed[2] from the blockchain-data-structure and their transactions will be added to the inbox to be processed again.

12. The node whose block was accepted will receive the fees for all transactions contained in the block as reward.

13. If a block is removed from the blockchain-data-structure, then the reward for adding it is withdrawn from the node that initially received it.

---

[2]Blocks that are identified as invalid later on are actually not physically removed from the blockchain-data-structure. Instead, they are marked as invalid and treated as if they had been removed. As a result, all changes are retained as documented.

Why It Works

The reasons the preceding rules work are:

- Due to rule 1, all nodes receive all information needed to validate and add transaction data.

- Due to rule 2, nodes process new transaction data they receive.

- Due to rule 3, the blocks created by other nodes are processed immediately on arrival at the nodes inbox.

- Due to rule 4, only valid transaction data are added to the blockchain-data-structure.

- Due to rule 5, all nodes take part in a race for solving the hash puzzle. Due to the nature of the hash puzzle it is unpredictable which node will solve it first.

- Due to rule 6, all nodes are informed when a node solves the hash puzzle of a new block.

- Due to rules 6 and 3, all nodes receive the newly created block and recognize the winner of the race for solving the hash puzzle.

- Due to rule 7, all nodes of the system review and verify newly created blocks and ensure that only correct blocks are accepted.

- Due to rule 8, all nodes add new blocks to their own copy of the blockchain-data-structure and hence grow the transaction history.

- Due to rule 9, the collectively maintained transaction history is kept free of invalid transactions and hence maintains integrity.

- Due to rule 10, no transaction data will be added twice.

- Due to rule 11, no valid transaction will get lost even if previously processed blocks are reprocessed.

- Due to rule 11, the system is able to perform ex post validity checks on the transaction history and correct it retrospectively.

- Due to rule 12, nodes have an incentive to process transactions and to create new blocks quickly.

- Due to rule 12, all nodes have an incentive to inform all other nodes about a new block because earning a reward depends on having transactions examined and accepted by all other nodes.

- Due to rule 13, nodes have an incentive to work correctly, to avoid accepting any invalid transaction data, or producing invalid blocks.

- Due to rule 13, nodes have an incentive to review and revalidate blocks and transactions in a retrospective way.

Dealing with Dishonest Behavior

The blockchain aims to create integrity and trust in a completely open peer-to-peer system that is made up of an unknown number of nodes with unknown reliability and trustworthiness. The most prominent kinds of dishonest behavior in peer-to-peer systems that manage ownership are:

- Submitting transactions by pretending to be someone else

- Accepting invalid transaction data or blocks

- Overwhelming a node with many transaction data with the goal to make it crash

- Refusing to process certain transaction data

- Refusing to forward information

All of these cases of dishonest behavior are already covered by:

- The security concept of the transactions (identification, authentication, and authorization via asymmetric cryptography and digital signatures) that restricts access to an account to the owner of the corresponding private key

- The gossip communication model that ensures that every node eventually receives all information

- The architecture of the system that ensures that the whole system stays alive even if some individual nodes crash or stop processing data

- The blockchain-algorithm

The most important weapon of the blockchain against dishonest nodes is the power of the honest majority and the effects of reward and punishment. Even if some nodes send forged transactions or accept invalid transaction data or invalid blocks, the majority of honest nodes and their striving for reward will outweigh the attempts of the dishonest to counteract the integrity of the system. Clearly, this approach depends on the assumption that there really is a majority of honest nodes.

Outlook

This step explained how the blockchain processes transaction data and adds them to the blockchain-data-structure and thereby includes them in the official history of transaction data. The instructions discussed in this step are supposed to ensure that all nodes in the system maintain identical versions of the blockchain-data-structure and hence maintain the identical history of transaction data. However, sometimes nodes maintain different histories, and this means they do not agree on one identical history of transaction data. Resolving these conflicts is another task of the blockchain-algorithm, which will be considered in the next step.

Summary

- The blockchain-algorithm is a series of rules and instructions that governs the way in which transaction data are processed and added to the system.

- The challenge solved by the blockchain-algorithm is to keep the system open to everyone while ensuring that only valid and authorized transactions are added.

- The blockchain-algorithm utilizes the carrot-and-stick approach, combined with competition and peer control.

- The major idea of the blockchain-algorithm is to allow all nodes of the system to act as supervisors of their peers and reward them for adding valid and authorized transactions and for finding errors in the work of others.

- Due to the rules of the blockchain-algorithm, all nodes of the system have an incentive to process transactions correctly and to supervise and point out any mistakes made by the other peers.

- The blockchain-algorithm is based on the following concepts:

  - Validation rules for transaction data and block headers

  - Reward for submitting valid blocks

- Punishment for counteracting the integrity of the system

- Competition among peers for earning reward based on processing speed and quality

- Peer control

- The rules of the competition establish a two-step rhythm that governs the work of every node in the network. At any given point in time, all nodes of the system are in either of the two phases:

  - Evaluating a new block that was created by others

  - Trying hard to be the next node that creates a new block that has to be evaluated by all others

- The working rhythm is imposed by the arrival of messages at the individual nodes.

- The majority of honest nodes and their striving for reward will outweigh the attempts of dishonest nodes to counteract the integrity of the system.

Choosing a Transaction History

Let computers vote with their feet

Step 18 explained how the nodes of the blockchain process transaction data and new blocks. However, the transaction history maintained by the individual nodes of the system may still differ due to delays or errors in message passing. Hence, this step focuses on resolving conflicts among the different versions of the transaction history maintained by the individual nodes of the system.

The Metaphor

When was the last time you took a walk through a park? Have you noticed a phenomenon that can be observed in most parks all over the world? They have paved paths that were created based on the plans and ideas of landscape architects, and there are also beaten paths created by visitors. Often these beaten paths are straight lines across the lawn and provide efficient shortcuts between two landmarks, two park benches, or other points of interest. Beaten

© Daniel Drescher 2017
D. Drescher, *Blockchain Basics*, DOI 10.1007/978-1-4842-2604-9_19

paths emerge at places where many people independently and consistently decide to walk off the paved paths because doing so appears to be more desirable than following the paved path. Hence, the creation of dirt paths in parks can be seen as the result of a very basic form of democracy. There are no official polls or elections that rule the creation of these paths, instead every visitor contributes to their emergence with his or her own independent decision to walk or not to walk along certain paths and to leave his or her footprints on the ground. Less-often–used beaten paths disappear as nature takes back its territory, but others remain since many people continue to walk on them. This learning step explains an aspect of the blockchain that functions similar to the emergence and disappearance of beaten paths in parks.

The Goal

The goal is to maintain one unambiguous history of transaction data among all nodes in the network that as a result yields identical outcomes when clarifying ownership requests, regardless of the specific node being contacted or requested.

The Challenge

The blockchain-algorithm as explained in Step 18 imposes a two-step rhythm to all nodes of the system. At any given point in time, each node of the system is either examining a new block that was created by one of their peers or trying hard to be the next node that creates a new block that subsequently has to be examined by all others. However, there is no global clock that rules the nodes and stipulates which of the two kinds of work has to be done at any given time. The arrival of new blocks at the inboxes of the individual nodes is the clock-pulse generator that governs the work of any given node. However, the arrival of new blocks at the inboxes of the individual nodes is highly influenced by the message delivery capabilities of the network, which has its own adversities. Messages may get lost, may be delivered with time delay, or may arrive in any order. As a result, the nodes of the network do not have the identical information at their disposal at the same time. Furthermore, the switch between the two working phases does not take place at the identical time for all the nodes. Instead, each node switches between the two working phases at its own individual time governed by the arrival of messages in its inbox. This causes an overlap of the working phases of the individual nodes. Both effects impose a huge obstacle toward maintaining one unambiguous history of transaction data among all peers in the network. Hence, the challenge is to find a way to identify one unambiguous history of transaction data in the face of all message delivery adversities and without falling back to a centralized solution.

The Idea

The example of beaten paths in parks shows that a group of people can reach agreement or consensus in collective decision-making problems by independently and consistently voting with their feet. The result of that kind of voting is often called distributed consensus because is its reached among independently acting individuals without a central element of control or coordination.

Note   Consensus is a synonym for an agreement among independent individuals. Distributed consensus is an agreement among the members of a purely distributed peer-to-peer system.

Situations in which a crowd or swarm of independently acting individuals solves a collective problem can be characterized by the following conditions[1]:

1.   A group of individuals operate in the identical environment.

2.   A collective decision-making problem exists.

3.   The individuals independently strive to achieve an identical goal.

4.   The individual actions performed to achieve one's goal leave visible marks in the environment that help to decide the collective decision-making problem.

5.   The individuals use identical criterion for evaluating the decision-making problem based on the alteration of their environment.

The idea of the blockchain is to let all nodes independently vote with their feet and thereby reach a collective agreement regarding the selection of one version of the transaction history. The blockchain as we know it at this point of the book fulfills the first four conditions of collective decision making:

1.   All nodes operate in the identical environment consisting of the network, nodes that maintain their individual copies of the blockchain-data-structure, and the blockchain-algorithm that governs the behavior of the nodes.

2.   The decision-making problem is to select one transaction history collectively.

---

[1]Hassanien, Aboul Ella, and Eid Emary. *Swarm intelligence: Principles, advances, and applications.* Boca Raton, FL: CRC Press, 2016.

3.   All nodes strive to maximize their individual income earned as reward for adding new valid blocks to the blockchain-data-structure.

4.   In order to achieve their goals, all nodes send their new blocks to all their peers to have them examined and accepted. As a result, each node leaves its individual footprint in the environment that is the collectively maintained blockchain-data-structure.

However, a fifth point is missing: a criterion that all nodes use for making a decision based on the alteration of their environment. The idea of how to select a history of transaction data is based on how new blocks are added to the blockchain-data-structure and how the data are protected against manipulation. Due to the proof of work, adding a new block is computationally expensive and makes attempts to manipulate the transaction history even more computationally expensive. Hence, the amount of aggregated computational effort spent on creating a transaction history seems to be a natural criterion for selecting a history of transaction data in the case that more than one conflicting version exists. If all nodes of the system apply the identical criterion for selecting a transaction history, then all nodes of the system eventually agree on the identical version of the history. The collectively selected version of the transaction history is often called the authoritative chain or history.

How It Works

The idea of selecting a transaction history based on the computational effort that was spent for creating it has led to the following two criteria:

- The longest-chain-criterion[2]
- The heaviest-chain-criterion[3]

The Longest-Chain-Criterion

The longest-chain-criterion is based on the idea that the blockchain-data-structure that comprises the most blocks represents the most aggregated computational effort. In order to study this criterion, let's consider an initial situation were all the nodes of a distributed system maintain and agree on

---

[2]Nakamoto, Satoshi. Bitcoin: A peer-to-peer electronic cash system. 2008. https://bitcoin.org/bitcoin.pdf.
[3]Wood, Gavin. Ethereum: A secure decentralized generalized transaction ledger. 2014. http://gavwood.com/paper.pdf; Okupski, Krzysztof. Bitcoin developer reference. Working paper. 2014.

the identical version of the blockchain-data-structure, as depicted in Figure 19-1, which presents a schematic blockchain-data-structure that omits many details for simplicity. Each of the boxes represents one block that is identified with a shortened hash value. The arrow that points from one box to another represents the hash reference that links a block header to its predecessor. In this initial situation, all nodes agree on one history of the transaction data and strive for extending the existing chain with another block that refers to block A397 as its predecessor.

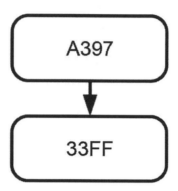

Figure 19-1. Initial blockchain-data-structure in a distributed system

Finding a new block is a race among all nodes because it requires the solution of the block-specific hash puzzle. Figure 19-2 shows the blockchain-data-structure that the *majority* of nodes maintain after one node solved the hash puzzle of a new block and sent it to its peers. As a result, those nodes that maintain a blockchain-data-structure as depicted in Figure 19-2 strive to extend it with a new block that refers to block AB12 as its predecessor. From the majority point of view, only one version of the blockchain-data-structure consisting of three blocks exists. However, sending a new block through a network costs time and it encounters all sorts of adversaries. Due to a delay in the message passing, a minority of nodes have not received block AB12 yet. Hence, they still try to extend the chain depicted in Figure 19-1. Eventually, one of them successfully solves the hash puzzle for a new block with the hash value DD01 and passes it to its peers. Eventually, the majority of nodes have received both block AB12 and block DD01. As a result, the majority of nodes maintain a blockchain-data-structure as depicted in Figure 19-3, which consists of two branches on top of a common trunk. In such a situation, the longest-chain-criterion does not yield an unambiguous result because both chains (AB12 → A397 → 33FF and DD01 → A397 → 33FF) have the same length.

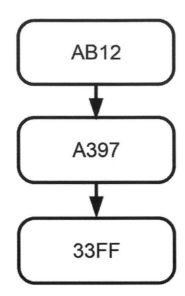

Figure 19-2. Result of adding a new block to the existing blockchain-data-structure

In the situation presented in Figure 19-3, the nodes are free to decide which branch to extend.

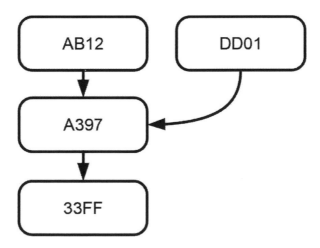

Figure 19-3. The blockchain-data-structure after a delayed block was delivered

Some nodes may strive to find a new block that refers to block AB12 as its predecessor, while other nodes strive for finding a new block that refers to block DD01 as its predecessor. Suddenly, the majority of nodes receive two new blocks, BB11 and CCC1, which both refer to block AB12 as its predecessor. This can happen due to two nodes finishing the proof of work for their blocks nearly at the same time. The result of incorporating these two new blocks into the blockchain-data-structure is a data structure that contains three chains, as shown in Figure 19-4. One of the chains only consists of three blocks, while the other two consist of four blocks.

The longest-chain-criterion clearly rules out the shortest chain, which is the chain DD01 → A397 → 33FF. However, the longest-chain-criterion does not yield an unambiguous result because there are two chains of the same length. As a result, some nodes may strive to find a new block that refers to block BB11 as its predecessor, while other nodes may strive to find a new block that refers to block CCC1 as its predecessor.

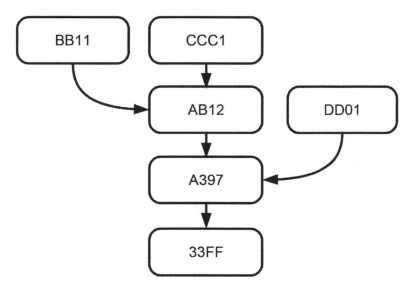

Figure 19-4. A blockchain-data-structure after two nodes finish the proof of work at nearly the same time

Eventually, one new block arrives that refers to block BB11 as its predecessor, which yields the data structure as depicted in Figure 19-5. The blockchain-data-structure depicted in Figure 19-5 contains many conflicting versions of the transaction history, but the longest-chain-criterion yields one unambiguous result that is the chain consisting of the blocks 0101 → BB11 → AB12 → A397 → 33FF. The majority of nodes and eventually all nodes of the system will use that chain for clarifying ownership-related requests. The majority of nodes and eventually all nodes of the system will strive to extend this branch by finding a new block that refers to block 0101 as its predecessor.

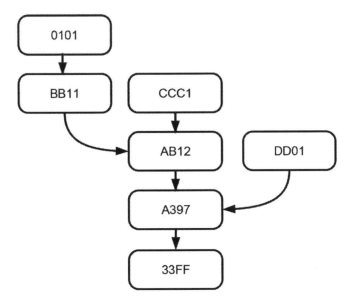

Figure 19-5. Schematic illustration of a blockchain-data-structure that contains one longest chain after a new block arrived

An important result is that the blockchain-data-structure actually does not look like a straight chain, instead it looks more like a tree or a columnar cactus, a blockcactus so to speak. The branches of the tree represent conflicting versions of the transaction history, but based on the longest-chain-criterion, all nodes eventually identify the identical version of the transaction history consentaneously.

▓ **Note** Due to its shape, the blockchain-data-structure is often referred to as a tree-data-structure. The very first and therefore oldest block in the blockchain-data-structure is the one that has no predecessor, and it is often called the root of the tree-shaped structure. A block without a successor is called the leaf. A straight sequence of blocks from the root to a leaf is called the path.

The Heaviest-Chain-Criterion

In Step 16 you learned that blockchain applications rarely utilize a constant difficulty level for the hash puzzle to be solved for adding a new block to the blockchain-data-structure. Instead, they typically determine the difficulty level dynamically, which causes the blocks to differ with respect to the computational effort that was spent for adding them to the blockchain-data-structure. On the other hand, the longest-chain-criterion is based on the idea that the path that contains the most blocks is the one that represents the most computational effort. However, in the case of heterogeneous difficulty levels, the longest path is not necessarily the one that represents the most computational effort.

For each path, the computational effort that was spent upon it can be measured by adding up the difficulty level of all blocks that belong to it. This value can be calculated by utilizing the fact that the block header contains the difficulty level of its hash puzzle. The aggregated difficulty level of a path is often called its weight. Figure 19-6 depicts the identical blockchain-data-structure as shown in Figure 19-5 but this time it also shows the difficulty level for each of its blocks. The longest chain (the path from root 33FF to leaf 0101) has a weight of 5, while the second-longest chain (the path from root 33FF to leaf CCC1) has a weight of 6. Hence, the blockchain-data-structure depicted in Figure 19-6 illustrates the situation where the longest-chain-criterion will cause the nodes to select a chain that does not represent the most computational effort.

As a result, blockchains that determine the difficulty level dynamically do not utilize the longest-chain-criterion. Instead, they utilize the heaviest-chain-criterion: they select that history of transaction data, which is represented by the heaviest chain. In the case that the difficulty level is identical for all blocks, the longest path is identical with the heaviest path and both the longest-chain-criterion and the heaviest-chain-criterion yield the identical result.

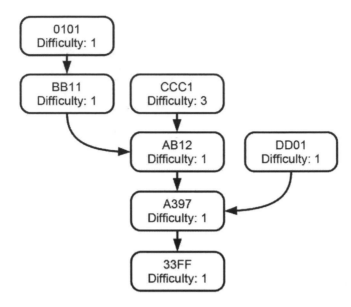

Figure 19-6. Schematic illustration of a blockchain-data-structure with difficulty levels

Consequences of Selecting One Chain

Selecting one specific chain among conflicting versions and establishing it as the authoritative chain has the following consequences:

- Orphan blocks
- Reclaimed reward
- Clarifying ownership
- Reprocessing of transactions
- A growing common trunk
- Eventual consistency
- Robustness against manipulations

Orphan Blocks

The blockchain-data-structure that is grown collectively looks like a tree whose branches represent different conflicting versions of the transaction history. Applying a selection criterion actually means selecting one path of that tree and establishing it as the authoritative version of the history of transaction data. All blocks in the tree-shaped data structure that are not part of the authoritative path are abandoned by the nodes and are called orphan blocks.[4] For example, when applying the longest-chain-criterion to the situation depicted in Figure 19-4, the block DD01 is an orphan block, while in Figure 19-5, the blocks DD01 and CCC1 are not part of the longest chain and are abandoned. When applying the heaviest-chain-criterion to the situation depicted in Figure 19-6, the blocks 0101, BB11, and DD01 are not part of the authoritative chain and therefore are abandoned.

Reclaimed Reward

Orphan blocks are useless for the purpose of clarifying ownership, as they do not contribute to the authoritative chain. As a result, the reward given to the node that created and submitted them is reclaimed. This is due to rule 11 and rule 13 of the blockchain-algorithm as explained in Step 18, which state that if a block that was added to the blockchain-data-structure is identified as invalid or useless later on, that block as well as all its subsequent blocks will be logically removed from the blockchain-data-structure and the reward that was given for adding it is withdrawn from the node that initially received it.

Clarifying Ownership

Only those transactions that are part of the authoritative chain are considered to have happened and are used to clarify ownership-related requests. Orphan blocks are not part of the collectively selected chain. Hence, their transaction data are not part of the history of the transaction data. Instead they are considered as if they never happened, and they are treated as nonexistent when it comes to clarifying ownership-related requests.

Reprocessing of Transactions

Transaction data that are part of orphan blocks were originally submitted with the goal of adding them to the transaction history. The fact that they are treated as if they never happened was never planned beforehand, instead, it is the result of the random nature of the proof of work and its role in growing the blockchain-data-structure. Transaction data that unluckily ended up in orphan blocks are given another chance to become part of the selected transaction history by putting them in the node's inbox again to be reprocessed and added to the blockchain-data-structure later on. This is due to rule 11 of the blockchain-algorithm, as explained in Step 18. As a result, transactions that were once part of the authoritative chain can disappear for a while if the majority of nodes abandon the block to which they belong, but they will appear later as soon as they have been reprocessed.

---

[4]Okupski, Krzysztof. Bitcoin developer reference. Working paper. 2014.

A Growing Common Trunk

Applying a selection criterion does not always yield an unambiguous result. For example, in situations such as those depicted in Figure 19-3 and Figure 19-4, more than one longest chain exists. In these situations, the blockchain-data-structure has two equal length paths that arise from a common trunk. In Figure 19-3, the common trunk consists of just two blocks that form a short chain A397 → 33FF. In Figure 19-4, the common trunk already consists of three blocks that form the chain AB12 → A397 → 33FF, which includes the common trunk of the previous situation. Hence, even if a selection criterion yields ambiguous results, the conflicting versions of the transaction history arise from a less ambiguous common trunk. The deeper down the blockchain you look, the less ambiguous the decision whether or not a block is part of the longest chain.

Eventual Consistency

Let's consider the situation depicted in Figure 19-4, where the longest-chain-criterion does not yield an unambiguous result. As you can see in Figure 19-5, the next block being added to the blockchain-data-structure determines whether block BB11 or CCC1 will either be part of the longest chain or be abandoned instead. But who decides that the next block being added to the blockchain-data-structure shown in Figure 19-4 refers to block BB11 as its predecessor and hence abandons block CCC1? The surprising and maybe disappointing answer is that it is purely random. In the situation shown in Figure 19-4, the nodes are free to decide which branch to extend. As a result, some nodes may strive to find a new block that refers to block BB11 as its predecessor, while other nodes may strive to find a new block that refers to block CCC1 as its predecessor. Which of them finishes the new block first depends on the solution of the hash puzzle, which takes a finite but random length of time. The node that solves the hash puzzle of a new block first decides which of the conflicting branches gets extended and which blocks get abandoned. Hence, the growth of the tree-shaped blockchain-data-structure exhibits a random behavior due to the speed race for solving the hash puzzle and the random fluctuations in messages passing through the network. The next block, whose time of appearance is governed by the random duration needed to solve its hash puzzle, determines which of the paths will be extended and which block will be abandoned.

As previously discussed, conflicting branches of the tree-shaped blockchain-data-structure share a common trunk that stays constant regardless of the blocks or leafs that are abandoned. Hence, the blocks located at or near the top of the authoritative chain are most affected by the random nature of the arrival of new blocks, while blocks deeper down in the blockchain-data-structure are less affected. Hence, it can be stated: The *deeper down* the authoritative chain a block is located:

- The *further in* the past it was added
- The *more time* has passed since its inclusion in the blockchain-data-structure
- The *more common effort* has been spend on adding subsequent blocks
- The *less it is* affected by random changes of the blocks that belong to the longest chain
- The *less likely* it will be abandoned
- The *more accepted* it is by the nodes of the system
- The *more anchored* it is in the common history of the nodes

The fact that certainty concerning the inclusion of blocks in the authoritative chain increases as time goes by and more blocks are added eventually is called *eventually consistency*.

Robustness Against Manipulations

That path of the tree-shaped blockchain-data-structure that represents the most computational effort is the authoritative version of the transaction history. Establishing and maintaining the authoritative path is just a matter of controlling the majority of the computational power of the whole system. Establishing a new authoritative path that starts at one of the inner blocks of the blockchain-data-structure requires catching up with and overtaking the path maintained by the majority. This fact is the basis for the robustness of the blockchain.

As long as honest nodes own the majority of computational resources of the whole system, the path maintained by them will grow fastest and outpace any competing paths. In order to manipulate an inner block, an attacker would have to redo the proof of work of that block and subsequently redo the hash puzzle of all blocks after it and then catch up with and overtake the path maintained by the honest nodes[2]. However, establishing a new path by catching up with and overtaking the path maintained by the majority is impossible for any attacker that controls less computational power than the majority. Hence, any attempt to establish a new authoritative path that contains fraudulent transactions will be outpaced and therefore abandoned by the path that is maintained by the honest majority. As a result, the history of transactions maintained by the system is robust against manipulations.

Threats to the Voting Schema

Any procedure of collective decision making will be the target of manipulations if it appears to be worthwhile to influence the outcome of the whole process. The blockchain and its distributed consensus algorithm is no exception to that. There are many discussions about how the blockchain consensus algorithm can be manipulated. Regardless of how diverse these manipulations may appear, they have only one goal: turning blocks that are part of the authoritative chain into orphan blocks and establishing a new authoritative chain that represents a history of transaction data and an alternative distribution of ownership rights that is more favorable from the attackers point of view.

However, one can discuss these manipulations from a variety of viewpoints. Economically, these manipulations try to change the allocation of ownership rights by changing the collective history of transaction data. Regarding collective decision making, these manipulations try to gather the majority of voting power in order to enforce a desired result. From a technical point of view, any attempt to manipulate the collective decision-making process aims to undermine the integrity of the system. Regarding the distributed nature of the system, these manipulations try to establish, at least temporarily, a hidden element of centrality that changes the state of the system. Hence, these attacks are often called 51 percent attacks.

Note A 51 percent attack is an attempt to gather or control the majority of the whole voting power in a collective decision-making process.

The Role of the Hash Puzzle

In Step 16 you learned how to make the blockchain-data-structure immutable. Hence, from a purely technical point of view, the hash puzzle is just a means to an end to make the blockchain-data-structure immutable. However, when you consider the usage of the blockchain-data-structure, another aspect of the hash puzzle is seen. In the course of reaching a collective agreement regarding the transaction history, the individual blocks that make up the blockchain-data-structure can be seen as a voting ballot, while the hash puzzle can be seen as a price that makes submitting a ballot costly and hence detains the dishonest from taking part in the vote.

Any attempt to manipulate the collective decision-making process of the blockchain aims to gather the majority of the voting power. Due to the fact that the blockchain binds voting power on computational power via the hash puzzle, any attempt to gather the majority of voting power actually means gathering the majority of the computational power of the whole peer-to-peer system. The reliability and trustworthiness of the way the blockchain reaches collective agreement relies on the assumption that no single person or entity can acquire or gather the majority of accumulated computational power of the whole peer-to-peer system.

Why It Works

Building up the blockchain-data-structure collectively is a bit like taking part in a continuous voting schema. Each single node has only a tiny voice in the ongoing poll about which transaction history should be chosen, but all nodes together form a powerful population that consistently selects its own history. This works because taking part in the ongoing voting scheme is neither without costs nor is it unaccommodating. Taking part in the vote costs work necessary to solve the hash puzzle, and by submitting a vote or a new block, a node commits itself to it in order to receive a reward. Since all nodes independently utilize the identical criterion for selecting a transaction history, eventually all nodes reach a consensus.

Outlook

This step focused on the way the nodes of a purely distributed peer-to-peer system reach an agreement concerning the collectively maintained history of transaction data and highlighted the importance of the hash puzzle for reaching consensus and maintaining integrity. The next step discusses the importance of reward and the instrument of payment used to compensate the peers for contributing to the integrity of the system.

Summary

- Delays in sending new blocks across the network or two nodes creating new blocks nearly at the same time cause the blockchain-data-structure to grow into the shape of a tree or a columnar cactus with branches that arise from a common trunk that represent conflicting versions of the transaction history.

- Selecting an identical version of the transaction history is a collective decision-making problem.

- Distributed consensus is an agreement among the members of a purely distributed peer-to-peer system in a collective decision-making problem.

- The collective decision-making problem of the blockchain is characterized by the following facts:

  - All nodes operate in the identical environment, consisting of the network, nodes that maintain their individual copies of the blockchain-data-structure, and the blockchain-algorithm that governs the behavior of the nodes.

  - The decision-making problem is to select the identical transaction history across all nodes.

  - All nodes strive to maximize their individual income earned as a reward for adding new valid blocks to the blockchain-data-structure.

  - In order to achieve their goals, all nodes send their new blocks to all their peers to have them examined and accepted. As a result, each nodes leaves its individual footprint in the environment that is the collectively maintained blockchain-data-structure.

  - All nodes use the identical criterion for selecting a history of transaction data.

- The longest-chain-criterion states that each node independently chooses the path of the tree-shaped blockchain-data-structure that contains the most blocks.

- The heaviest-chain-criterion states that each node independently chooses that path of the tree-shaped blockchain-data-structure that has the highest aggregated difficulty.

- Selecting one path of the tree-shaped blockchain-data-structure has the following consequences:

  - Orphan blocks

  - Reclaimed reward

  - Clarifying ownership

  - Reprocessing of transactions

  - A growing common trunk

- Eventual consistency

- Robustness against manipulations

- The deeper down the authoritative chain a block is located:

  - The further in the past it was added

  - The more time has passed since its inclusion in the blockchain-data-structure

  - The more common effort has been spent on adding subsequent blocks

  - The less it is affected by random changes of the blocks that belong to the longest chain

  - The less likely it will be abandoned

  - The more accepted it is by the nodes of the system

  - The more anchored it is in the common history of the nodes

- The fact that certainty concerning the inclusion of blocks in the authoritative chain increases as time goes by and as more blocks are added eventually is called eventually consistency.

- A 51 percent attack is an attempt to gather or control the majority of the whole voting power in a collective decision-making process with the goal to turn blocks that are part of the authoritative chain into orphan blocks and establish a new authoritative chain that contains a transaction history that is more favorable from the attackers point of view.

- A 51 percent attack has the following characteristics:

  - Economically: Changing the allocation of ownership rights by changing the collective history of transaction data.

  - Decision making: Gathering the majority of voting power in order to enforce a desired result.

  - Technically: Undermining the integrity of the system.

  - Architecturally: Establish at least temporarily a hidden element of centrality that changes the state of the system.

Paying for Integrity

Neither integrity nor the creation of trust is without costs

The discussion of how the blockchain processes new transaction data and how the nodes of the system reach an agreement concerning the true history of transactions revealed the importance of the hash puzzle. Solving the hash puzzle plays an important role in achieving and maintaining the integrity of the system. But solving the hash puzzle costs computational resources and, as a consequence, it costs money. For that reason, it is necessary to compensate the nodes that contribute to the integrity of the system for doing so. However, throughout the discussion, it has been assumed that the nodes are compensated somehow without asking which instrument of payment is used to do so. Hence, this step focuses exclusively on how nodes are compensated for their contribution to the integrity of the system.

The Metaphor

Let's imagine you are the owner of a bakery. One day you come up with a great idea on how to improve your business. You realized that money is scarce, but you always have bread for sale in your bakery, and at the end of

© Daniel Drescher 2017

D. Drescher, *Blockchain Basics*, DOI 10.1007/978-1-4842-2604-9_20

most business days there is a significant amount of bread left over. Hence, you decide to pay your employees with bread instead of paying them money. This will accomplish two things: save you money and avoid the need to throw away leftover bread. Your employees are not excited about this idea, but soon other companies imitate you and finally all companies begin to apply this compensation schedule: car manufacturers pay their employees with cars, construction companies pay their employees with houses, and so on. One day your friends are complaining about their impractical compensation, except for one of them who is still getting paid with money. Which company or institution do you think this person works for? It turns out that he works for a central bank, which happens to be a producer of money!

This example plays with the dependency between the goods we create by fulfilling our jobs and the goods we receive as compensation. This step discusses that connection in the context of the blockchain. It will turn out that under some conditions it may become desirable for the blockchain to become more like a central bank that pays its employees with the bank notes it produces. But before I discuss this special case, let's review in more detail the role of fees and the importance of compensation within the blockchain.

The Role of Fees Within the Blockchain

Step 18 highlighted that the blockchain utilizes the carrot-and-stick approach in order to get the peers that make up the system control one another. Competition for reward and threat of punishment are the two forces that keep peers of the system verifying transactions orderly and selecting that transaction history that unites the most collective effort. Reward and punishment are implemented with rewards based on transaction fees and proof of work.[1] This effect is universal in all blockchain applications regardless of their concrete application goal. However, the choice of a concrete instrument of payment used to compensate the maintainers of the system is not identical in all blockchain applications. Defining and using an instrument of payment that will be given to the peers for verifying and adding new blocks to the blockchain is considered one of the major challenges in establishing a blockchain application. As a result, the following consequences of choosing an instrument of payment have to be considered:

- The impact on the integrity of the system

- The impact on the openness of the system

- The impact on the distributed nature of the system

- The impact on the philosophy of the system

---

[1]Nakamoto, Satoshi. Bitcoin: A peer-to-peer electronic cash system. 2008. https:// bitcoin.org/bitcoin.pdf.

Impact on the Integrity of the System

The forces of reward and punishment are the foundation of achieving and maintaining integrity in the blockchain. This works because the peers of the system receive a valuable compensation for maintaining the integrity of the system. But how do we know that the peers indeed receive a valuable compensation for their work in the first place? Well, that is the whole point. Which instrument of payment is considered valuable and worthwhile for doing the work of maintaining the system? What happens if this instrument of payment is known to lose its value or is not trustworthy? Can we expect that the peers who maintain the blockchain will continue doing so when they are compensated with an untrustworthy and worthless instrument of payment? No, we cannot. Lack of trust in the instrument of payment used to compensate the peers of the system will contaminate the whole system. Hence, the instrument of payment used for compensating the supporters of the system directly impacts the trustworthiness of the blockchain itself.

Impact on the Openness of the System

The blockchain is supposed to be an open peer-to-peer system. Everyone can connect his or her computer to the system and will be rewarded for contributing to the maintenance of its integrity. But what happens if the instrument of payment used to compensate peers is not as open as the blockchain itself? What if the compensation is done by using an instrument of payment that is available or accepted only in specific countries or is subject to capital movement restrictions? In this case, the instrument of payment counteracts the technical openness of the system by inducing economic constraints.

Impact on the Distributed Nature of the System

The blockchain is a purely distributed peer-to-peer system without any element of central control or coordination. But what happens if the instrument of payment used to compensate peers is controlled and governed by one central institution? This means allowing centrality to enter the system through the back door. It would counteract the distributed nature of the system.

Impact on the Philosophy of the System

The preceding discussion revealed that the properties of the instrument of payment used to compensate peers for supporting the system have the potential to counteract major aspects of the blockchain. This raises a fundamental question: How can a purely distributed peer-to-peer system that is designed to stay free of centralized control be considered credible if it uses an instrument of payment to compensate its peers that counteracts its major values? Every blockchain that claims to be completely open and purely distributed has to find a satisfying answer to this question.

Desirable Properties of an Instrument of Payment for Compensating Peers

In order to interfere as little as possible with the goals and values of the blockchain, an instrument of payment to be used for compensating peers should:

- Be available in digital form; otherwise it cannot be included in the blockchain.

- Be accepted as an instrument of payment in the real world; otherwise peers cannot use their income from supporting the system to pay their bills in the real world.

- Be accepted as an instrument of payment in all countries; otherwise supporting the system will become unattractive to peers who live in those countries that do not accept it as an instrument of payment.

- Not be subject to capital movement restrictions; otherwise its transfer to peers is restricted.

- Have a stable value; otherwise the peers have an economic risk of losing purchasing power.

- Be trustworthy; otherwise it undermines the ability of the blockchain to create trust.

- Not be controlled by one single central organization or state; otherwise it causes a serious conflict to the distributed nature of the blockchain.

This list of properties reads like a wish list for the perfect world currency. Hence, it is no surprise that none of the existing fiat currencies fulfills these desired properties.

A Detour to the Emergence of Cryptographic Currencies

The previous section listed desired properties of an instrument of payment for compensating peers of a blockchain. The finding that none of the existing fiat currencies fulfills these properties is a bit sobering because they are desirable in their own right. A currency or an instrument of payment that has these properties would also be useful in many occasions other than compensating peers of a distributed system. It turns out that many people have already thought about that problem. The first and most prominent blockchain application was formed to solve this problem. The idea of that blockchain is brilliant: It is a purely distributed peer-to-peer system that manages ownership of a new kind of digital money, which, in turn, is used to compensate the peers of the system for verifying and adding new blocks to the blockchain-data-structure. This particular new money connects its application goal, the management of ownership of a new kind of money, with the need to have a trustworthy instrument of payment for compensating its contributors. I am talking about Bitcoin. The Bitcoin system not only manages ownership of the new digital money in a purely distributed peer-to-peer system but it also compensates its peers with the money to whose integrity they contribute. Due to the fact that the blockchain relies heavily on cryptography, this new kind of money is also called cryptographic money or cryptocurrency for short. As a rule of thumb, you could say that Bitcoin and many other cryptographic currencies are like bakeries that pay their employees with the bread they produce, with the difference being that the bread they produce is actually a new digital currency.

Outlook

This step highlighted the importance of the instrument of payment used to compensate the peers of the blockchain. This step is the last of a series of steps, which focus on the fundamental principles of the blockchain individually. The next step will bring all the pieces together and summarize what you have learned in the preceding learning steps.

Summary

- The blockchain utilizes fees for compensating its peers for contributing to the integrity of the system.
- The instrument of payment used to compensate peers has an impact on major aspects of the blockchain such as:
  - Integrity
  - Openness
  - The distributed nature
  - The philosophy of the system

- Desirable properties of an instrument of payment for compensating peers are:

  - Being available in digital form

  - Being accepted in the real world

  - Being accepted in all countries

  - Not being the subject to capital movement restrictions

  - Being trustworthy

  - Not being controlled by one single central organization or state

- A cryptocurrency is an independent digital currency whose ownership is managed by a blockchain that uses it as an instrument of payment for compensating its peers for maintaining the integrity of the system.

Bringing the Pieces Together

More than just the sum of its pieces

This step is the summit of this book's intellectual journey toward an understanding of the blockchain. While Steps 9-20 explored the individual concepts that make up the blockchain in isolation, this step brings all these pieces together. As a result, you will gain not only an understanding of the blockchain as a whole but also see how the different concepts work together. This learning step starts with reviewing the major concepts and technologies of the blockchain and continues with an explanation about what the blockchain is based on the technical knowledge gained in the previous steps. Finally, this step provides a review of the definition of the blockchain-technology-suite, which conse-quently opens the blockchain to a wide range of application areas.

Reviewing Concepts and Technologies

The intellectual journey toward an understanding of the blockchain started in Step 8 where we planned the design of a purely distributed peer-to-peer system for managing ownership. Table 21-1 presents these tasks, their goals, the corresponding steps, and the corresponding concepts of the blockchain.

© Daniel Drescher 2017
D. Drescher, *Blockchain Basics*, DOI 10.1007/978-1-4842-2604-9_21

Table 21-1. Review of the Tasks of Designing a Distributed Peer-to-Peer System for Managing Ownership

Task Number	Goal	Step Number	Major Concept
1	Describing Ownership	9	History of Transaction Data
2	Protecting Ownership	10–13	Digital Signature
3	Storing Transaction Data	10, 11, 14, 15	Blockchain-Data-Structure
4	Preparing Ledgers for Being Distributed	16	Immutability
5	Distributing Ledgers	17	Information Forwarding in Networks
6	Adding New Transactions	18	Blockchain-Algorithm
7	Deciding Which Ledger Represents the Truth	19	Distributed Consensus

It is important to understand that these major concepts that make up the blockchain rely on other concepts and technologies. Understanding the blockchain requires at least an appreciation of these concepts as well. For that reason, Table 21-2 summarizes on a more detailed level the technologies that make up the blockchain. The remainder of this step draws on the concepts exhibited in these two tables.

Table 21-2. Technical Concepts of the Blockchain, Their Purpose, and Metaphor

Concept	Purpose	Metaphor Used
Transaction Data	Describing transfer of ownership	Bank transfer form
Transaction History	Proving the current state of ownership	The course of a relay race
Cryptographic Hash Value	Identifying any kind of data uniquely	Human fingerprints
Asymmetric Cryptography	Encrypting and decrypting data	Public mailbox with lock
Digital Signature	Stating agreement with the content of transaction data	Handwritten signature
Hash Reference	A reference that becomes invalid once the data being referred are changed	Cloakroom tickets that utilize hash values for identifying cloak hooks
Change-Sensitive Data Structures	Storing data in a way that makes any manipulation stand out immediately	Jackets that carry cloakroom tickets in their pockets

(continued)

Table 21-2. (continued)

Concept	Purpose	Metaphor Used
Hash Puzzle	Imposing a computationally expensive task	Opening a number lock by trial and error
Blockchain-Data-Structure	Storing transaction data in a change-sensitive way and maintaining their order	A library with a card catalog
Immutability	Making it impossible to change the history of transaction data	Attempt to establish a fake family history
Distributed Peer-to-Peer Network	Sharing the transaction history among all nodes of a network	Groups of independent witnesses
Message Passing	Ensure that all nodes of the system eventually receive all information	Gossip among people
Blockchain-Algorithm	Ensure that only valid transaction data are added to the blockchain-data-structure	Carrot-and-stick approach to ruling contractors
Distributed Consensus	Ensure that all nodes of the system use the identical history of transaction data	Beaten path in a park as a result of visitors voting with their feet
Compensation	Giving nodes an incentive to maintain integrity	Bakery that pays its employees with bread

What Is the Blockchain?

After gaining an overview of the individual concepts that make up the blockchain, it is important to see how they work together. The approach of analyzing systems by identifying functional and nonfunctional aspects of their application and implementation layer provides support for tackling the challenge of understanding how the concepts of the blockchain work together. Table 21-3 provides an overview of the layers and the aspects of the blockchain, which will guide you in bringing the concepts together.

Table 21-3. Layers and Aspects of the Blockchain

Layer	Functional Aspects	Nonfunctional Aspects
Application	Clarifying ownership	Highly available
	Transferring ownership	Reliable
		Open
		Pseudoanonymous
Implementation	Ownership logic	Secure
	Transaction security	Resilient
	Transaction processing logic	Eventually consistent
	Storage logic	Keeping Integrity
	Consensus logic	
	Purely distributed peer-to-peer architecture	

The Purpose of the Blockchain: Functional Aspects of the Application Layer

The blockchain serves two purposes:

- Clarifying ownership
- Transferring ownership

Clarifying Ownership

Clarifying ownership means answering the major question that constitutes ownership, which is: Who owns what amount of what object at what time?

Transferring Ownership

Transferring ownership means changing the current state of ownership. With regard to this purpose, the blockchain lets owners transfer their property to someone else. Hence, it answers another major question for proving ownership, which is: Who has transferred ownership of what by which amount to whom at what time?

Properties of the Blockchain: Nonfunctional Aspects

When interacting with the blockchain, you will notice how it fulfills its duties. The quality at which the blockchain serves its purpose is described by its nonfunctional aspects:

- Highly available
- Censorship proof
- Reliable
- Open
- Pseudoanonymous
- Secure
- Resilient
- Eventually consistent
- Keeping integrity

Highly Available

The blockchain does not have a downtime. Instead, the blockchain is available all the time 24 hours a day, 7 days a week, the whole year all the time. It does not even have a switch off button.

Censorship Proof

There is no one who individually dictates the content of the blockchain or can switch off the whole system.

Reliable

The blockchain fulfills its purpose consistently with a good quality. One can trust the blockchain in clarifying and transferring ownership correctly.

Open

The blockchain does not exclude certain users or computers from utilizing its services. Instead, it is open to everyone.

Pseudoanonymous

The blockchain identifies owners uniquely but it neither maintains nor reveals their real-world identity.

Secure

The blockchain is secure in two aspects: (1) on the level of individual transactions, (2) on the level of the whole system. Regarding the individual level, the blockchain ensures that ownership is kept exclusive to the disposal of the lawful owner only. On the overall level, the blockchain protects the ownership of all owners from manipulation, forgery, counterfeiting, double spending, and unauthorized access.

Resilient

The blockchain is able to clarify and transfer ownership correctly even under difficult conditions. The blockchain withstands a wide range of attacks on ownership such as forgery, double spending, counterfeiting, and accessing ones property by pretending to be someone else.

Eventually Consistent

The blockchain will not yield consistent results all the time. Instead, the chance of getting consistent results will increase over time and will eventually reach full consistency throughout the whole system.

Keeping Integrity

The blockchain maintains its integrity by displaying behavior that is free of logical errors. It maintains data consistency and ensures security on the level of individual transactions and the whole history of transaction data.

Internal Functioning: Functional Aspects of the Implementation Layer

The internal functioning of the blockchain can be traced back to the following major components:

- Ownership logic
- Transaction security
- Transaction processing logic
- Storage logic
- Peer-to-peer architecture
- Consensus logic

Ownership Logic

The ownership logic governs how ownership is clarified and transferred. The blockchain utilizes individual transaction data for describing the transfer of ownership and maintains the whole transaction data for clarifying ownership. Figure 21-1 illustrates the ownership logic and its underlying concepts. Concepts shown by boxes on the top depend on those below them. The very bottom row of boxes exhibits the concepts on which the ownership logic depends and that need to be specified further.

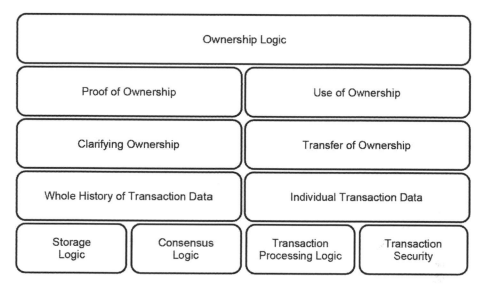

Figure 21-1. Ownership logic and its underlying concepts

The ownership logic utilized by the blockchain relies on a storage logic that maintains the whole history of transaction data and a consensus logic that ensures its consistency. Additionally, the ownership logic relies on a transaction processing logic that ensures that only valid transaction data are added to the data store and transaction security that ensures that only the lawful owner can transfer his or her property to another account. These four concerns are addressed by the remaining components of the blockchain.

Transaction Security

Transaction security ensures that only the lawful owner can access and transfer his or her ownership to another account. Figure 21-2 illustrates the concepts involved in implementing transaction security. Basic concepts such as cryptographic hash values and asymmetric cryptography are located in boxes at the very bottom since they serve as the foundation for all other concepts located in boxes above them. For example, digital signature is located below authorization because it is a measure to authorize a transaction, but it is located above cryptographic hash values and private key since it utilizes these concepts. In a similar fashion, Figure 21-2 makes the dependence between authentication and identification on lower-level cryptography more obvious.

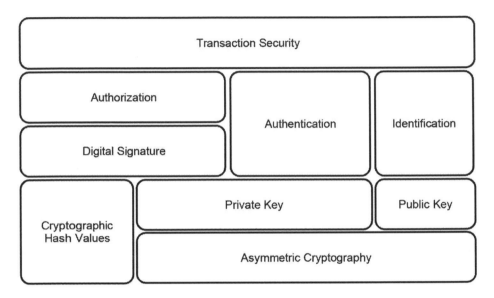

Figure 21-2. Transaction security and its underlying concepts

Transaction Processing Logic

The transaction logic ensures that only valid transaction data are added to the collectively maintained history of transaction data. It clearly depends on the validation of transaction data that represent the genuine goal of the system. Every single node of the system in isolation can do the validation of transaction data. However, a single node could make errors in validating transaction data or it could accept invalid transaction data on purpose. Both cases are threats to the integrity of the whole system. For that reason, the processing of transactions involves a sophisticated mechanic containing the validation of new blocks or its headers, respectively: peer-to-peer architecture and peer control and competition, which in turn rely on the forces of reward and punishment. Figure 21-3 depicts the relation of these concepts by presenting them in boxes that are built on top of one another to point out their dependence.

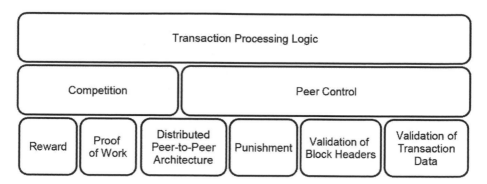

Figure 21-3. Transaction processing logic and its underlying concepts

Storage Logic

The processing of valid transactions results in them being added to the whole history of transaction data, which means adding them to a data store that maintains the whole history of transaction data. The integrity of the whole system and its ability to fulfill its purpose of clarifying and transferring ownership relies on the integrity of this data store. Hence, the storage logic is concerned with maintaining the whole history of transaction data and protecting them from being manipulated, forged, or counterfeited by pursuing the idea of making changes to data prohibitive expensive. As illustrated by Figure 21-4, the storage logic achieves this by maintaining an immutable append-only data store that is based on the proof of work and the blockchain-data-structure. Its functioning can be traced back to hash puzzles, hash references, and change-sensitive data structures, which in turn can be traced back to the basic concept of cryptographic hash values. Figure 21-4 depicts the dependence of the storage logic by layering derived concepts on top of boxes that represent more basic concepts.

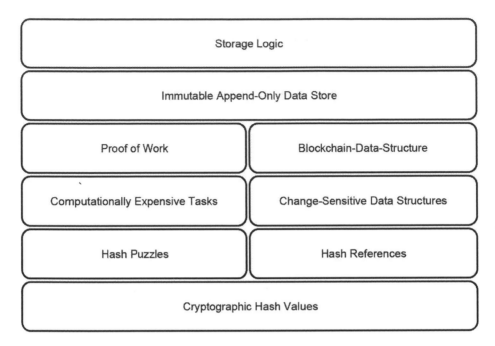

Figure 21-4. Storage logic and its underlying concepts

Peer-to-Peer Architecture

The architecture determines how the components or nodes of the system are related and connected with one another. As illustrated in Figure 21-5, the blockchain utilizes a purely distributed peer-to-peer system that consists of independent peers called nodes. These nodes are connected with one another via a network that serves as a medium for communication. Each of the peers maintains its own copy of the blockchain-data-structure containing the whole history of transaction data. The peers communicate with one another by utilizing a gossip-style message-passing protocol that ensures that eventually each peer will receive all of the information.

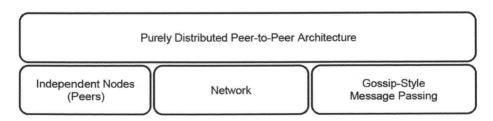

Figure 21-5. Architecture and its underlying concepts

Consensus Logic

Since all the nodes of the distributed system maintain their history of transaction data independently, their content can differ due to delays or other adversities of passing messages through a network. As a result, the data store that was meant to form a straight line of linked data blocks actually forms a three-shaped data structure where each branch represents a conflicting version of the transaction history. The consensus logic as depicted in Figure 21-6 makes all nodes of the system eventually consistent by making them choose the identical version of the transaction history that unites the most collective effort.

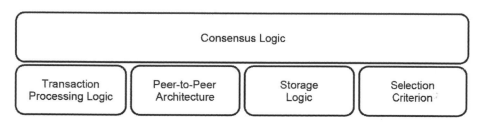

Figure 21-6. Consensus logic and its underlying concepts

Gaining Abstraction

Abstraction is gained by identifying and distinguishing the components of the blockchain that are specific to the goal of managing ownership from those that are agnostic to the specific application goal. This is consistent with our under-standing of the blockchain-technology-suite, as discussed in Step 5. Evidently, the ownership logic and transaction data are components that are specific to the application, since they determine how ownership is described with trans-action data and how ownership is clarified and transferred. On the other hand, transaction security and the transaction procession logic are less specific to the application goal. The former utilizes the generic concepts of identifica-tion, authentication, authorization, and digital signatures that can be used in any other application as well. As shown in Figure 21-3, the latter is a huge data processing apparatus whose majority of components are agnostic to the application goal. The only component of the transaction processing logic that is tightly coupled with the application goal is the validation of transaction data. All other components such as competition, peer control, reward, punishment, and the validation of block headers are agnostic to the specific data being pro-cessed. Figure 21-7 illustrates the result of distinguishing application-specific components of a blockchain from those that are agnostic to the specific appli-cation goal, which in turn form the blockchain-technology-suite.

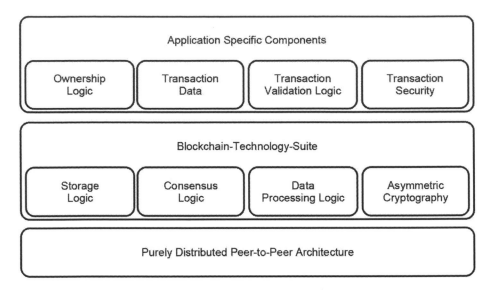

Figure 21-7. The blockchain-technology-suite within the blockchain

Outlook

This step focused on bringing all of the pieces of the preceding steps together in order to gain an overview of the blockchain. The openness and the absence of any form of central control or coordination are the foundation of the system as they allow its nodes to act as independent witnesses for clarifying ownership-related matters. However, these characteristics may also cause unwanted consequences. What these unwanted consequences are and how they may limit the use of the blockchain will be discussed in the next step.

Summary

- The blockchain is a purely distributed peer-to-peer system that addresses the following aspects of managing ownership:

  - Describing ownership: History of Transaction Data

  - Protecting ownership: Digital Signature

  - Storing transaction data: Blockchain-Data-Structure

  - Preparing ledgers for being distributed: Immutability

  - Distributing ledgers: Gossip-Style Information Forwarding Through a Network

- Processing new transactions: Blockchain-Algorithm

- Deciding which ledger represents the truth: Distributed Consensus

- Analyzing the blockchain involves the following aspects:

  - The application goal

  - Its properties

  - Its internal functioning

- The blockchain has two application goals:

  - Clarifying ownership

  - Transferring ownership

- The blockchain fulfills its application goals while exhibiting the following qualities:

  - Highly available

  - Censorship proof

  - Reliable

  - Open

  - Pseudoanonymous

  - Secure

  - Resilient

  - Eventually consistent

  - Keeping integrity

- Internally the blockchain consists of components that are either specific or agnostic to the application goal of managing ownership.

- The application-specific components of the blockchain are:

  - Ownership logic

  - Transaction data

  - Transaction processing logic

  - Transaction security

- The application-agnostic components are:
  - The blockchain-technology-suite
  - The purely distributed peer-to-peer architecture
- The blockchain-technology-suite consists of:
  - Storage logic
  - Consensus logic
  - Data processing logic
  - Asymmetric cryptography

Limitations and How to Overcome Them

This learning stage focuses on the major limitations of the blockchain, the reasons they occur, and the possible ways to overcome them. By the end of this stage, you will understand why the original idea of the blockchain that was explained in the previous steps may not be suitable for large-scale commercial applications and what changes have been suggested to overcome these limitations as well as their consequences. Finally, this stage will familiarize you with the terminology used to refer to the major variations of the blockchain.

Seeing the Limitations

Even a perfect machine has limitations

Step 21 brought all the pieces together and yielded an overview of the blockchain as a whole, highlighting the interdependency of its underlying technical concepts. As a result, we concluded that the blockchain is a complex and highly sophisticated technical construct. One can state without exaggeration that it is the masterpiece of an ingenious mind. However, the blockchain is neither perfect nor free of limitations. Hence, this step highlights and explains major limitations of the blockchain and why these limitations cause significant hurdles for its commercial use. Finally, this step sketches how the limitations of the blockchain can be overcome.

The Challenge

The blockchain is a purely distributed peer-to-peer system that allows everyone to read the transaction history and add new transaction data to the collectively maintained data store. The openness and the absence of any form of central control or coordination are the foundation of the system as they allow its nodes to act as independent witnesses for clarifying ownership-related matters. However, openness and the absence of central control may have unwanted consequences that limit the usability of the system. Hence, the challenge is to identify and understand the consequences of the system in order to formulate strategies to overcome them.

© Daniel Drescher 2017
D. Drescher, *Blockchain Basics*, DOI 10.1007/978-1-4842-2604-9_22

Technical Limitations of the Blockchain

The most important technical limitations of the blockchain are:

- Lack of privacy
- The security model
- Limited scalability
- High costs
- Hidden centrality
- Lack of flexibility
- Critical size

Lack of Privacy

The blockchain is a purely distributed peer-to-peer ledger that maintains the whole history of transaction data. All transaction details such as the goods and the amount being transferred, the involved accounts, and the time of transfer are accessible to everyone.[1] This is necessary in order to allow every peer to clarify ownership and to verify new transactions (e.g., by identifying double-spending attacks). Hence, the lack of privacy is a constituting element of the blockchain. Without that level of transparency, the blockchain could not fulfill its duty. However, this level of transparency is often regarded as a limiting factor for application cases that require more privacy.

The Security Model

The blockchain utilizes asymmetric cryptography for identification, authentication of users, and for authorizing transactions. Account numbers in the blockchain are actually public cryptographic keys. Only the one who possesses the corresponding private key can access the property that is associated with an account. Only transaction data that contain a digital signature that was created with the corresponding private key are valid and can transfer property from one account to another one. The private key is the only security instrument that authorizes the lawful owner. As soon as the private key of an account is given to some else, either on purpose, by accident, by mistake, or due to data robbery, the security for that individual account is broken.

---

[1]Nakamoto, Satoshi. Bitcoin: A peer-to-peer electronic cash system. 2008. `https:bitcoin.org/bitcoin.pdf`.

There are no additional security measures that protect the property that is associated with an account number. It is important to point out that the asymmetric cryptography used in the blockchain is considered as being among the best and strongest cryptographic methods available. Hence, there is no failure or flaw in the security concept of the blockchain per se. However, there is no additional safety net to protect the users of the blockchain from losing or unwillingly share their private key with others. This is similar to the way security keys are used in real life to protect houses or cars or the way in which PIN numbers are used to secure credit or debit cards. Once you give someone the key, regardless of the circumstances or the reason why that happened, the security is broken and anyone who has the PIN or the key can withdraw money from your credit card or can drive away with your car. The private key of a blockchain account is no exception to that. However, some people consider the lack of additional security measures a limiting factor for the usage of the blockchain.

Limited Scalability

The blockchain is a peer-to-peer system that aims to achieve two goals: on the one hand, it allows everyone to add new transaction data to the collectively maintained history; on the other hand, it ensures that the history of transaction data is protected from being manipulated or forged. The blockchain balances both goals by utilizing an immutable append-only data structure that requires the solution of a hash puzzle every time a new block is added. Solving that hash puzzle is time consuming on purpose. Insisting on the solution of the hash puzzle is an appropriate way to make attempts to manipulate the history of transaction data prohibitive costly. Unfortunately, this security measure comes at the price of reduced processing speed and hence limited scalability. This characteristic of the blockchain is considered a serious hurdle for using it in contexts that require high processing speed, high scalability, and high throughput.

High Costs

The issue of high costs is related to the problem of limited scalability. Solving the hash puzzle or providing the proof of work is computationally expensive on purpose. It is the security measure that makes the history of transaction data immutable. The computational costs can be expressed in a variety of scales such as the number of computational cycles, physical time, electrical energy, and money. However, the result is always the same: The proof of work is expensive. Hence, the whole blockchain incurs costs. The magnitude of these costs depends on the difficulty of the hash puzzles.

Hidden Centrality

The requirement to solve a hash puzzle for each block being added to the blockchain-data-structure and the rules for distributing rewards for contributing to the integrity of the system cause a race of arms among the peers. Those who have the necessary financial resources invest in specialist hardware that makes solving the hash puzzle and hence contributing to the system profitable.[2] On the other hand, the venture of validating and adding new transaction data to the system becomes unprofitable for those without access to specialist hardware, which as a consequence causes them to withdraw from contributing computational resources to the system. As a result, the supposedly large and diverse group of peers that collectively maintains the integrity of the system eventually becomes a very small group of entities that each owns huge computational power in the form of specialist hardware. The remaining group of peers forms an oligopoly that divides the responsibility of maintaining the integrity of the system among themselves. Similar to oligopolies in other industries, this small group of entities could abuse its power (e.g., by omitting specific transactions or discriminating specific users). This effect establishes a kind of hidden centrality that undermines the distributed nature of the whole system.[3] From a technical point of view, such a system is still a distributed system, but it is a system whose integrity is maintained by only a small number of entities.

Lack of Flexibility

The blockchain is a complex technical construct that consists of a variety of concepts and protocols that are optimized and adopted to one another. Changing that fine-tuned ecosystem can be very challenging. Actually, there is no established procedure for how to change or upgrade major components of a blockchain once it has started its operation. This implicitly constitutes a long service life for the technologies that make up the blockchain. For example, the cryptographic procedures have to be valid for the lifetime of the blockchain, which is potentially centuries. This is also true for the blockchain-algorithm and how conflicts are resolved. There is also a problem for people developing on the blockchain caused by immutability, in that it is difficult to fix bugs or make adjustments to the blockchain protocol. These characteristics make the whole blockchain-technology-suite less flexible than other technologies.

---

[2]Taylor, Michael Bedford. Bitcoin and the age of bespoke silicon. In *Proceedings of the 2013 International Conference on Compilers, Architectures and Synthesis for Embedded Systems.* Montreal: IEEE Press, 2013.

[3]Kroll, Joshua A., Ian C. Davey, and Edward W. Felten. The economics of Bitcoin mining, or Bitcoin in the presence of adversaries. Proceedings of WEIS. 2013.

Critical Size

The robustness against manipulations and hence the trustworthiness of the collectively maintained history of transaction data rely on the assumption that the majority of the system's computational power is controlled by honest nodes. However, in small peer-to-peer systems with a limited computational power, that majority can still be very small, which in turn could make it possible to perform a 51 percent attack. This problem is in particularly relevant for cryptocurrencies with low market capitalization and limited user adoption. Hence, any blockchain will require a critical mass of honest nodes to support it and make it resistant to attackers with a lot of computational power. Reaching a critical size that makes 51 percent attacks impossible is a challenge that every new blockchain has to face.

Nontechnical Limitations of the Blockchain

The most important nontechnical limitations of the blockchain are:

- Lack of legal acceptance
- Lack of user acceptance

Lack of Legal Acceptance

The blockchain is a technology that offers its users the possibility to manage and transfer ownership in an open and purely distributed peer-to-peer system. The way independent peers manage ownership collectively through a distributed consensus has raised questions concerning the legal consequences of transactions being made and managed in the blockchain. Questions regarding the legal implications and acceptance of transactions performed in the blockchain need to be discussed regardless of the safety, security, and sophistication of its technology. It is a question regarding the incorporation of a new approach of managing ownership in the established legal system. Those who witnessed the emergence and development of the Internet may see a similarity between legal statuses of the blockchain nowadays and the lack of legal acceptance of Internet commerce in the 1990s.

Lack of User Acceptance

User acceptance, or a lack of it, is another limitation that cannot be underestimated. An open legal status of the blockchain will cause uncertainty among its users, which in turn will reduce their interest in using it. An additional aspect of user acceptance is knowledge and education. It is unrealistic to expect that customers will use and trust the blockchain when its fundamental functioning is not understood.

Overcoming the Limitations

Both the technical and the nontechnical limitations are considered major hurdles for the adoption of the blockchain in real-world applications. How to overcome particular limitations has been, and still is, an area of active research and further developments. A detailed discussion of these activities is beyond the scope of this book. However, the following sections sketch how to overcome the limitations of the blockchain.

Technical Limitations

Overcoming the technical limitations of the blockchain may require interventions on all components and technical levels. One of the major challenges in overcoming technical limitation of the blockchain is the distinction between improving its technology and changing its technology fundamentally. The next step discusses this subject in more detail.

Nontechnical Limitations

The nontechnical limitations of the blockchain can be seen as social, economic, legal, and psychological aspects of adapting to a new technology. Education and legal initiatives can be seen as the appropriate measures to master the adoption of the blockchain. The example of the Internet and e-commerce has already shown that it takes time to answer legal questions that come with new technologies and that it takes time for users to understand, trust, and use them. Fortunately, the case of the Internet and e-commerce has also illustrated that educational initiatives about the functioning of a new technologies increase its acceptance and adoption among users and foster the solution of legal issues.

Outlook

This step highlighted major technical and nontechnical limitations of the blockchain that can be regarded as hurdles for its adoption. Educational and legal initiatives can be seen as a way to overcome the nontechnical initiatives of the blockchain. The next step focuses on overcoming some of the technical limitations.

Summary

- The openness of the blockchain and the absence of any form of central control are the fundamentals of its functioning but can also cause limitations for its adoption.

- Major technical limitations of the blockchain are:

  - Lack of privacy

  - The security model

  - Limited scalability

  - High costs

  - Hidden centrality

  - Lack of flexibility

  - Critical size

- The most important nontechnical limitations of the blockchain are:

  - Lack of legal acceptance

  - Lack of user acceptance

- Technical limitations of the blockchain can be overcome by improving the existing technology or by introducing conceptual changes.

- The nontechnical limitations of the blockchain can be overcome by educational and legislative initiatives.

Reinventing the Blockchain

The emergence of four different kinds of blockchain

Step 22 highlighted the major limitations of the blockchain and sketched possible approaches to overcome them. This step goes a bit further in analyzing two of the major technical limitations of the blockchain. It explains the root of the major technical limitations of the blockchain and explains how they have been overcome. This step will also explain the emergence of four distinct versions of the blockchain and their differences and discusses the consequences of the emergence of these versions of the blockchain.

The Metaphor

Oftentimes we try to achieve two or more goals that cannot be fulfilled at the same time, such as doing work quickly and correctly or driving fast and safe. The incompatibility between two or more opinions or goals is called a conflict, which can be solved either by finding a compromise or by deciding in favor of one option to the disadvantage of all alternatives. This step presents two major conflicts of the blockchain that are represented in two of its major technical limitations and how the attempt to overcome them led to the invention of four distinct versions of the blockchain.

© Daniel Drescher 2017
D. Drescher, *Blockchain Basics*, DOI 10.1007/978-1-4842-2604-9_23

Conflicting Goals of the Blockchain

The blockchain faces two conflicts:

- Transparency vs. privacy
- Security vs. speed

Transparency vs. Privacy

The blockchain clarifies ownership based on the whole history of transaction data, which is available to everyone. As a result, the blockchain is similar to a public transaction register or a public ledger. Being open and transparent is the core concept of the blockchain for verifying ownership. This openness is the foundation of solving the double-spending problem because everyone can audit everyone else's transactions and hence can uncover double-spending attacks easily.

However, this approach is in contrast to the concept of privacy. Privacy means keeping transaction data or details of them such as the involved accounts or the amount being transferred hidden from the public. Hence, the resulting conflict is between the transparency needed for clarifying ownership, on the one hand, and higher privacy requirements of its users, on the other hand.

Security vs. Speed

Without exaggeration, it can be stated that the history of transaction data is the heart of the blockchain. The history of transaction data is protected from being manipulated and forged by storing it in an immutable append-only blockchain-data-structure, which requires the solution of a hash puzzle for every block being added or rewritten. This not only makes it prohibitively costly to manipulate or forge the history of transaction data but also slows down the speed at which new transaction data can be added to the blockchain-data-structure. This is in contrast to the speed and scalability requirements of many applications in a commercial context. Hence, the resulting conflict is between securing the history of transaction data based on a time-consuming proof of work, on the one hand, and speed and scalability requirement of its users, on the other hand.

The Roots of the Conflicts

The roots of the two conflicts are two fundamental operations of the blockchain: reading and writing transaction data. The conflict of openness vs. privacy can be traced back to the operation of reading the blockchain-data-structure, while the conflict of security vs. speed can be traced back to the operation of writing data to the blockchain-data-structure. Table 23-1 summarizes the relation between the two major technical limitations, the underlying conflict, and the corresponding fundamental functionality of the blockchain.

Table 23-1. Technical Limitations of the Blockchain and Their Reasons

Technical Limitation	Conflict	Fundamental Functionality
Lack of privacy	Transparency vs. privacy	Reading the history of transaction data
Lack of scalability	Security vs. speed	Writing transaction data to the data store

Solving the Conflicts

Conflicts can be solved either by finding a compromise that balances the competing goals or by enforcing one of the goals to the disadvantage of all others. The blockchain, as discussed so far, decided in favor of transparency and security to the disadvantage of privacy and speed. But there are alternative ways to solve these conflicts, which will be discussed in more detail in the following sections.

Deciding on Transparency vs. Privacy

Making a decision on the transparency vs. privacy conflict actually means deciding on whom to grant reading access. If only extreme cases of granting reading access are considered, there are two options: granting read access to everyone or granting read access only to a limited group of nodes or users. One can distinguish between the following types of blockchains that differ with respect to which users or nodes have the right to read the blockchain-data-structure and to create new transactions[1]:

- *Public blockchains* grant read access and the right to create new transactions to all users or nodes.

- *Private blockchains* limit read access and the right to create new transactions to a preselected group of users or nodes.

---

[1]BitFury Group. Public versus private blockchains Part 1: Permissioned blockchains. White paper, 2015. http://bitfury.com/content/5-white-papers-research/public-vs-private-pt1-1.pdf.

Deciding on Security vs. Speed

Making a decision for the security vs. speed conflict actually means to decide to whom you will grant writing access. If only extreme cases of granting writing access are considered, there are two options: granting writing access to everyone but making it computationally expensive by requiring the proof of work or restricting write access to a preselected group of users or nodes that were identified as trustworthy and requiring them to provide a less-expensive version of the proof of work. We can distinguish between the following types of blockchains based on granting write access[2]:

- *Permissionless blockchains* grant write access to everyone. Every user or node can verify transactions and create and add new blocks to the blockchain-data-structure.

- *Permissioned blockchains* grant write access only to a limited group of preselected nodes or users that are identified as trustworthiness through an on-boarding process. As a result, only the group of nodes that have write access are allowed to verify transactions and take part in the distributed consensus procedure.

Four Versions of the Blockchain

The decisions concerning reading and writing access can be made independently. Table 23-2 presents the four versions of the blockchain that arise when combining the extreme cases of reading and writing restrictions.

Table 23-2. Four Versions of the Blockchain as a Result of Combining Reading and Writing Restrictions

	Reading Access and Creation of Transactions	
Writing Access	**Everyone**	**Restricted**
Everyone	Public & Permissionless	Private & Permissionless
Restricted	Public & Permissioned	Private & Permissioned

---

[2]BitFury Group. Public versus private blockchains Part 2: Permissioned blockchains. White paper, 2015. http://bitfury.com/content/5-white-papers-research/public-vs-private-pt2-1.pdf.

The blockchain as defined in Step 5 and discussed throughout all the preceding steps is a public permissionless blockchain. Any restriction regarding reading or writing access to the blockchain-data-structure will yield one of the alternative versions. The most secretive version of the blockchain is the private permissioned blockchain. This version is the one that is considered the most useful in a commercial context because of its higher processing speed and its ability to hide transaction data from the public.

Consequences

Restricting reading or writing access to the history of transaction data impacts the following aspects of the blockchain:

- The peer-to-peer architecture
- The distributed nature
- The purpose

The Peer-to-Peer Architecture

In Step 3 you learned about peer-to-peer systems and their properties. One of the major features that is often considered the constituting characteristic of peer-to-peer systems is that they include computers that are all equal concerning their rights and roles. Although individual nodes may differ with respect to the resources they contribute, all the nodes in the system have the same functional capabilities and responsibilities. However, the four versions of the blockchain, as introduced above, differ with respect to granting reading and writing access to the nodes that make up the system. If nodes differ with respect to their ability to read or write transaction data, they are no longer equal. Hence, an important characteristic of peer-to-peer systems seems to be violated as a result of introducing restrictions on read and write access to the system.

The Distributed Nature

In Step 2 you learned about distributed systems and some of their properties. One of the major features that is often considered the constituting characteristic of distributed systems is the absence of any kind of central control or coordination. However, the emergence of the four different versions of the blockchain, as introduced above, is based on granting a preselected group of nodes or users read or write access to the history of transaction data while refusing these rights to all others. But who decides on granting or refusing reading or writing access to the system? Who makes the rules for granting or refusing reading or writing access?

If the rules that govern the allocation of reading and writing access are not administered and enforced by a purely distributed system, the system will have a central element, which in turn causes a contradiction to the distributed nature of the blockchain. The architecture of a presumably distributed system that utilizes a central element for administering and enforcing the rules that govern the allocation of reading and writing access could be depicted by the illustration shown in Figure 2-2. That means there is either a hidden element of centrality or the system appears as a centralized system to all nodes that have restricted access while utilizing a distributed system internally. In both cases, the whole system has more in common with a hybrid system consisting of distributed and centralized elements.

Purpose

In Step 4 you learned that the core problem to be solved by the blockchain is achieving and maintaining integrity in a purely distributed peer-to-peer system that consists of an unknown number of peers with unknown reliability and trustworthiness. Establishing restrictions on reading and writing access not only changes constituting properties of distributed peer-to-peer systems but also changes the trustworthiness of the nodes. If users or nodes that are allowed to write data to the blockchain-data-structure are evaluated regarding their trustworthiness beforehand in the course of an on-boarding process, the resulting environment may no longer consist of nodes whose trustworthiness is unknown. Hence, one may conclude that in such an environment the ability of the blockchain to create trust from an untrustworthy environment is no longer needed.

The blockchain causes value even in an environment that is made up of a known number of nodes with presumably known reliability and trustworthiness for the following reasons. First, the number of nodes in such a system can vary due to technical failures or downtime. Second, every distributed system faces the adversaries of networks that make communication on the level of individual messages unreliable. Finally, even an on-boarding process may not guarantee the trustworthiness of nodes at a 100 percent level. Additionally, even trustworthy nodes may yield wrong results due to technical failures.

Reviewing the Purpose of the Blockchain

Due to the consequences of imposing restrictions on the nodes on major aspects of the blockchain, we might revise our perception of its purpose. Imposing restrictions on reading and writing access may cause conflicts with the definition of the peer-to-peer system, the distributed nature of systems, and the purpose of the blockchain. However, the blockchain is also useful for maintaining integrity even in the most restricted case of a private permissioned blockchain. As a result, we may decide to relax the conditions under which the blockchain is supposed to create value. Instead of insisting that the blockchain's purpose is to maintain integrity of open and purely distributed peer-to-peer systems, we could state that its purpose is achieving and maintaining the integrity of distributed systems in general.

The Usage of the Term Blockchain in the Remainder of This Book

The remainder of this book continues with the use of the term blockchain in the sense of a public and permissionless system. In all other cases, it will be pointed out explicitly what kind of restricted blockchain is being considered.

Outlook

This step highlighted two approaches for overcoming two major technical limitations of the blockchain. It explained the emergence of four different kinds of blockchain with respect to the allocation of reading and writing access rights to the blockchain-data-structure. Up to this point of the book, the major ideas of the blockchain and its underlying concepts have been discussed. However, I have not discussed how it can be used in the real world. The next step will do that by considering both generic and more specific-use cases.

Summary

- The blockchain inherently contains the following conflicts:

  - Transparency vs. privacy: On the one hand, transparency is needed for clarifying ownership and preventing double spending, but on the other hand, its users require privacy.

  - Security vs. speed: On the one hand, protecting the history of transaction data from being manipulated is done by utilizing the computationally expensive proof of work, but on the other hand, speed and scalability are required in most commercial contexts.

- The transparency vs. privacy conflict has its root in the allocation of reading access rights to the blockchain-data-structure.

- The security vs. speed conflict has its root in the allocation of writing access rights to the blockchain-data-structure.

- Solving the transparency vs. privacy conflict led to the following versions of the blockchain:

  - Public blockchains grant reading access and the right to create new transactions to all users or nodes.

  - Private blockchains limit reading access and the right to create new transactions to a preselected group of users or nodes.

- Solving the security vs. speed conflict led to the following versions of the blockchain:

  - Permissionless blockchains grant writing access to everyone. Every user or node can verify transaction data and create and add new blocks to the blockchain-data-structure.

  - Permissioned blockchains grant writing access only to a limited group of preselected nodes or users that are identified as trustworthy through an on-boarding process.

- Combining these restrictions pairwise led to the emergence of four different kinds of blockchains.

- Restricting reading or writing access results in consequences on the following properties of the blockchain:

  - The peer-to-peer architecture

  - The distributed nature

  - Its purpose

- The blockchain-technology-suite causes value even in restricted environments for the following reasons:

  - The number of nodes can vary due to technical failures or downtime.

  - Every distributed system faces the adversaries of networks that make communication on the level of individual messages unreliable.

  - Even an on-boarding process may not guarantee the trustworthiness of nodes at a 100 percent level.

  - Even trustworthy nodes may yield wrong results due to technical failures.

Using the Blockchain, Summary, and Outlook

This stage concludes this intellectual journey through the blockchain. It considers how the blockchain can be used in real life, what generic use cases exist, and how to analyze existing blockchain applications. This stage also points out areas of active research and further developments. By the end of this stage, you will have gained a well-grounded understanding of major application scenarios of the blockchain, its most important advances, and its possible long-term accomplishments and disadvantages.

Using the Blockchain

A tool with thousands of applications

Steps 1 through 23 described what the blockchain is, what problem it solves, and how its works. However, the blockchain was not invented for the sake of busying ourselves with discussing its technological concepts. Instead, the blockchain was invented for use in the real world. Hence, this step explores in more detail how the blockchain can be used. It also describes generic application patterns of the blockchain and relates them to its properties. Additionally, this step sketches some specific applications of the blockchain and explains what details should be considered when analyzing a specific blockchain application.

The Metaphor

Why do people use shelves, cabinets, drawers, and boxes? These means of storage are widely used because they provide a way to store things and keep things tidy, regardless of their specific use. For example, one can use a box to store documents, technical spare parts, office supplies, photographs, money, DVDs, clothes, or wine bottles. The variety of the uses of boxes, drawers, cabinets, or shelves is only limited by the variety of the items that are stored in them. This learning step discusses the application of the blockchain by focusing

© Daniel Drescher 2017
D. Drescher, *Blockchain Basics*, DOI 10.1007/978-1-4842-2604-9_24

on the variety of the things that can be stored in it and the variety of contexts in which it can be used. But first I will review the properties of the blockchain as a special kind of box for digital items.

Characteristics of the Blockchain

The blockchain is a purely distributed peer-to-peer data store with the following properties:

- Immutable
- Append-only
- Ordered
- Time-stamped
- Open and transparent
- Secure (identification, authentication, and authorization)
- Eventually consistent

These properties of the blockchain are independent of the specific data stored in it. Hence, from a simplified point of view, we can consider the blockchain a special kind of box for storing digital items. This will open a huge variety of applications for the blockchain.

Generic Application Patterns

Based on the properties of the blockchain and its characteristic as being a generic data store for all kinds of data, we can come up with the following generic use cases:

- Proof of existence
- Proof of nonexistence
- Proof of time
- Proof of order
- Proof of identity
- Proof of authorship
- Proof of ownership

Proof of Existence

This use of the blockchain focuses on storing data for the sole purpose of proving its existence. Hence, this use utilizes neither the ordering nor the time-stamping capabilities of the blockchain. Concrete applications are, for example, registries of items that are supposed to be unique such as brand names, patents, license codes, and Internet or e-mail addresses.

Proof of Nonexistence

This use of the blockchain focuses on the opposite of the proof of existence. It provides ways to verify whether specific entries or items do not exist in the blockchain. Concrete applications of this could be records of complaints, fines, or convictions.

Proof of Time

In this case not only the sheer existence of an entry in the blockchain is important but also the time when the entry was added. The blockchain can serve that need since the blocks of the blockchain-data-structure store the time when the process of adding them was started. Applications that benefit from the time-stamping capabilities of the blockchain are those that track the occurrence of events in time such as delivery or notification tracking, tracking of payments, tracking of orderly opening and closing of public bidding procedures, and management of predictions.

Proof of Order

This pattern of usage utilizes the ordering capability of the blockchain. Applications that benefits from that property of the blockchain are those that track the relative ordering of events regardless of their absolute time, for example, tracking of application processes, auditing public bidding procedures, and escrow services. Proving that some event was the first or the last of its kind is a specific example of proof of order. This kind of proof can be important when resources are allocated in the same order in which certain claims or documents are submitted such as college or university applications, patent applications, or copyright claims.

Proof of Identity

Proof of identity can be considered a specific case of proof of existence because it proves that a certain identity already exists. The blockchain serves that use case since it not only stores data that can be used to identify someone or something but also provides basic security concepts for identification and authentication. Concrete applications of this use pattern are digital identity documents for people, animals, or goods. Governments could utilize such blockchains as part of their e-government strategy for managing personal documents, drivers' licenses, or passports.

Proof of Authorship

This use pattern focuses on proving that a specific person or institution added certain data to the blockchain. The blockchain can serve that purpose because it not only stores data that can be identified by its cryptographic fingerprint but also offers basic security concepts such as identification, authentication, and authorization. Identification and authentication are necessary to identify authors and verify their identity. Authorization is necessary in this use case in order to prevent someone from adding data to the blockchain without having the right to do so. Applications that utilize this use pattern are, for example, electronic publishing, tracking of content changes in documents, content delivery, collaborative editing, and protecting copyrights.

Proof of Ownership

This use pattern focuses on managing and clarify ownership. It relies on all previously mentioned patterns such as proof of existence, proof of order, proof of identity, and proof of authorship together with the three basic security concepts: identification, authentication, and authorization. Applications that utilize this use pattern are, for example, systems for managing ownership of real estate, cars, company shares, bonds, digital money, or cryptographic currencies.

Specific Use Cases

The blockchain is agnostic with respect to the data it stores. Hence, the range of data being stored in the blockchain and the range of its application areas are as wide and as diverse as human activities themselves. As a result, it is impossible to provide a complete overview of all blockchain applications. For that reason, this section presents a small selection of concrete blockchain application areas in which the blockchain is already used or may be used soon[1]:

- *Payments*: Managing ownership and transfer of digital fiat currencies.

- *Cryptocurrencies*: Managing ownership and creation of digital instruments of payment that exist independently from any government, central bank, or other central institution.

- *Micropayments*: Transfer of small amounts of money that would be too costly by using traditional means of transfer.

- *Digital assets*: Managing creation, ownership, and transfer of digital items that have value in their own right or represent valuable goods in the real world.

- *Digital identity*: Proving identity and authentication based on unique digital items.

- *Notary services*: Digitizing, storing, and verifying documents or contracts and proof of ownership or transfer.

- *Compliance and audit*: Auditing business activities of people or organizations in regulated industries in an audit track.

- *Tax*: Calculating and collecting taxes based on transactions or on sole ownership, reducing tax avoidance,[2] or double taxation.

- *Voting*: Creating, distributing, and counting digital ballot papers.

- *Record management*: Creation and storing of medical records.

---

[1] World Economic Forum. The future of financial services—How disruptive innovations are reshaping the way financial services are structured, provisioned and consumed. An Industry Project of the Financial Services Community, 2015; World Economic Forum. The future of financial infrastructure—An ambitious look at how blockchain can reshape financial services. An Industry Project of the Financial Services Community, 2016; Foroglou, George, and Anna-Lali Tsilidou. Further applications of the blockchain. 2015. Paper presented at the Columbia University PhD in Sustainable Development 10 Year Anniversary Conference, February 28, 2014.

[2] On the other hand, the use of truly anonymous cryptocurrencies may make tax avoidance easier.

Analyzing Blockchain Applications

Analyzing a blockchain application may become necessary in a variety of occasions such as becoming a customer of a company that uses the blockchain, investing in a blockchain startup, or using a blockchain application in your own company. In all of these cases, it needs to be decided whether a certain blockchain application is useful or whether it creates a tangible value. Since the blockchain is a complex technical construct, it may be challenging to get a clear view of the capabilities of the software system under consideration and to make a conscious purchase, investment, or usage decision. Hence, it may help to ask some or all of the following questions:

- What kind of blockchain is used?

- Are the requirements for using the blockchain fulfilled?

- What is the added value of using a distributed peer-to-peer system?

- What is the application idea?

- What is the business case?

- How are peers compensated for contributing resources to the system?

Are the Requirements for Using the Blockchain Fulfilled?

The blockchain is a purely distributed peer-to-peer system that consists of an unknown number of peers of unknown reliability and trustworthiness. Hence, the first point to be considered when analyzing a concrete blockchain application is its architecture and whether the architecture fulfills the conditions for applying the blockchain-technology-suite. It is important to find satisfactory answers to the following questions:

- What is the architecture of the system?

- What are the system components and how are they connected with one another?

- Is the system purely distributed or is there a central component whose failure can bring down the whole system?

- How do new nodes join the system?

- Can everyone join the system and start to contribute computational resources?

- Is there any kind of on-boarding process, due diligence process, or upfront security checking of new nodes that may establish a central element of control?

- Do all nodes have identical roles and rights in the system or do the nodes differ with respect to their rights to read or write data?

Answering these questions will help you to gain a basic understanding of the system and determine whether the blockchain-technology-suite is really needed. You could find out that the presumably blockchain system under consideration is a centralized system instead.

What Kind of Blockchain Is Used?

Not all distributed systems are open to everyone and grant reading and writing access to all their nodes. There are versions of the blockchain that differ with respect to the allocation of reading and writing access among the nodes. These differences have an impact on the architecture and the distributed nature of the system as well as on the purpose of the blockchain within those systems. Hence, it is important to find satisfying answers to the following questions:

- What kind of blockchain is used (public vs. private and permissioned vs. permissionless)?

- What rights are restricted?

- What groups of nodes have which rights?

- Why has the specific type of blockchain been chosen?

- Who decides which rights are given to what group of nodes?

- Who makes and enforces the rules regarding granting or refusing reading or writing access to the system?

- Who runs the on-boarding process?

- Are there any privacy or scalability concerns in the specific solution that could justify the restriction of certain rights?

What Is the Added Value of Using the Purely Peer-to-Peer System?

Both purely distributed peer-to-peer systems and centralized systems have their own advantages and disadvantages. Centralized systems are not inherently bad, they just pursue a different architectural concept that serves many application cases very well and still continues to do so. With some characteristics, centralized systems may be more desirable than distributed peer-to-peer systems. This is particularly true as integrity in purely distributed peer-to-peer systems is notoriously hard to maintain and costs additional effort. Hence, one needs good reasons for choosing a distributed peer-to-peer system over a centralized one. When analyzing a concrete blockchain application, it is important to find satisfying answers to the following questions:

- Why was the system implemented as a purely distributed peer-to-peer system in the first place?

- What are the alternatives?

- What are the advantages of utilizing a purely distributed peer-to-peer architecture over the alternatives and what are the disadvantages?

- What is the added value of using a distributed peer-to-peer architecture?

- Do the advantages of the peer-to-peer architecture outweigh the disadvantages?

Asking and insisting on the answers to these questions is important to distinguish those who consciously choose the distributed peer-to-peer architecture from those who use the blockchain just for the sake of using it.

What Is the Application Idea?

Analyzing the architecture of a system is important, but this does not yield answers concerning its application idea and how the system is supposed to create added value for its users. It is important to keep in mind that even the most sophisticated system architecture can never compensate for a weak or poor application idea. Excitement about the blockchain-technology-suite may make it easy to overlook a weak or poor application concept. Hence, when analyzing a blockchain application, it is important to find convincing answers to the following questions:

- What is the purpose of the application in the first place?

- What is the major problem domain of the system?

- Can the system be associated with specific industries or sectors and if yes what are they?

- What kind of service does the system offer to its users?

- What is the added value of using the system?

- What kind of generic blockchain use pattern does the system utilize?

- Are there any issues with the legal acceptance of the blockchain in the particular application area?

- What kinds of data are stored in the blockchain?

- What kinds of operations or transactions can be done?

- What kinds of security features are utilized?

- How do these aspects relate to the application idea of the system?

What Is the Business Case?

Another important aspect when analyzing blockchain applications is the commercial concept of the software system itself. The creation and operation of any software consume resources and hence cause costs. The blockchain is no exception to that. Analyzing the commercial conditions of blockchain software is an important step since many products or technical innovations fail due to flaws in their commercial concepts. Hence, it is necessary to find good answers to the following questions:

- What are the costs of purchasing or using the software?

- What are the fixed and variable costs of running or using the software?

- Who covers what costs?

- What license model is used?

- Who receives profits or who has to cover losses?

How Are Peers Compensated for Contributing Resources to the System and Maintaining Integrity?

The blockchain achieves integrity through the forces of reward and punishment implemented by income through fees and proof of work. Step 18 highlighted the importance of reward to compensate the contributors of the blockchain, while Step 20 pointed out the impact of the instrument of payment on the integrity, openness, and distributed nature of the system. Knowing and understanding how the peers are compensated for maintaining integrity is a crucial aspect in analyzing blockchain applications. Therefore, it is necessary to get satisfying answers to the following questions:

- What are the rules for compensating peers?

- Do the compensation rules together with the game theoretic aspects of the blockchain ensure and reward honesty to those who contribute to the system?

- What are the fees for having actions or transactions verified and executed by the system?

- What instrument of payment is used to pay transaction fees?

- What instrument of payment is used to compensate the peers for verifying and writing data in the blockchain?

Some blockchain applications use a cryptographic currency such as Bitcoin as an instrument of payment for fees and compensating peers. The resulting dependence on Bitcoin or another blockchain application may not be desirable in all circumstances.

Outlook

This step discussed aspects of applying the blockchain in the real world. However, I have not reached the point of finishing this discussion of the blockchain yet. The next step will summarize the learning path and point out areas for further development.

Summary

- The blockchain can be considered a purely distributed data store with additional properties such as being immutable, append-only, ordered, time-stamped, and eventually consistent.

- Being a generic data store means that the blockchain can store a wide range of data, which in turn makes it usable in a wide range of application areas.

- Based on its properties, we can identify the following generic-use patterns of the blockchain:
    - Proof of existence
    - Proof of nonexistence
    - Proof of time
    - Proof of order
    - Proof of identity
    - Proof of authorship
    - Proof of ownership
- Specific application areas of the blockchain that have already received attention or may receive attention in the future are:
    - Payments
    - Cryptocurrencies
    - Micropayments
    - Digital assets
    - Digital identity
    - Notary services
    - Compliance and audit
    - Tax
    - Voting
    - Record management
- When analyzing specific blockchain applications or blockchain services, some questions need to be answered:
    - What kind of blockchain is used?
    - Are the requirements for using the blockchain fulfilled?
    - What is the added value of using a purely distributed peer-to-peer system?
    - What is the application idea?
    - What is the business case?
    - How are peers compensated for contributing resources to the system?

Summarizing and Going Further

Further developments, alternatives, and the future of the blockchain

This step finishes this intellectual journey through the blockchain universe. After highlighting areas of further development and research, this step considers possible accomplishments of the blockchain within society. Before concluding with some comments about possible future trends in using the blockchain, this step also discusses some of its possible disadvantages.

© Daniel Drescher 2017
D. Drescher, *Blockchain Basics*, DOI 10.1007/978-1-4842-2604-9_25

The Metaphor

In 1994, a computer scientist and inventor described a software system he was about to develop[1]:

- *Decentralization*: No central authority and no single point of failure.

- *Nondiscrimination*: Everyone is free to choose his own way to connect to the system.

- *Openness*: The system will be developed in full view of everyone, encouraging maximum participation and experimentation.

- *Universality*: All the computers involved communicate with each other regardless of their hardware or location.

- *Consensus*: The system and its users will comply with standards that are created through a transparent participatory process based on consensus.

That list of properties reads like a short description of the blockchain. However, back in 1994, the blockchain did not exist! Actually, the system described by these points was the Internet, or at least Tim Berners-Lees's vision of the Internet.

As a result of technical progress, the emergence of Internet commerce, and the rise of Internet giants nowadays, the Internet may not have very much in common with Tim Berners-Lees's vision of the Internet formulated back in 1994. The fact that technology evolves and as a result diverges from the vision of its inventors should be kept in mind when considering the future of the blockchain. Hence, the evolution of the Internet could be considered a blueprint for the future evolution of the blockchain.

Further Developments and Alternatives

The blockchain is not a static construct that once developed remains unchanged for the rest of its existence. The blockchain as introduced and discussed in this book only provides the basis, which has already been and will continue

---

[1]World Wide Web Foundation. History of the Web. 2016. http://webfoundation.org/about/vision/history-of-the-web/.

to be the subject of research, improvements, and further developments.[2] Some of them can be seen as minor technical improvements, while others are conceptual chances or even radical advancements that may lead to separate and competing approaches. Without any claim to completeness, the following areas of improvement and further development should be noticed:

- Minor technical improvements and variations
- Improving scalability
- Conceptual evolutions and alternatives

Minor Technical Improvements and Variations

The blockchain utilizes a wide range of concepts and principles of software engineering and computer science such as hash functions, hash references, data structures, data storages, cryptography, network architectures, computer-to-computer communication, and computational puzzles. Each of these concepts and technologies has been and still is the area of active research. For example, there are a variety of hash functions, data structures, cryptographic procedures, communication protocols, and computational puzzles that can be used in a blockchain. As a result, we can create different versions of the blockchain just by utilizing different hash functions, cryptographic methods for creating keys, or computational puzzles used as proof of work. However, these variations have only a minor impact on the blockchain, as they do not alter its fundamental functioning; instead, they are only variations in some of its implementation details.

[2]Bonneau, Joseph, Andrew Miller, Jeremy Clark, Arvind Narayanan, Joshua A. Kroll, and Edward W. Felten. Research perspectives and challenges for Bitcoin and cryptocurrencies. In *IEEE Symposium on Security and Privacy*. IEEE, 2015, 104–121; Yli-Huumo, Jesse et al. Where is current research on blockchain technology?—A systematic review. *PloS One* 11.10 (2016), e0163477: doi:10.1371/journal. pone.0163477.

Improving Scalability

The major areas of research that focus on improving the scalability of the blockchain are network efficiency, storage, data usage, and the consensus algorithm.[3] Very promising approaches in this area are the lightning channel[4] and payment channels,[5] which allow commercially acceptable transaction times.

Conceptual Evolutions

Conceptual evolutions are real advancements in the way the blockchain works, what services it offers, or how users interact with it. The most important areas of conceptual evolutions of the blockchain are:

- Access rights
- Privacy
- Consensus
- Transactions
- Inventory data
- Data structure

Access Rights

Restricting reading or writing access to the blockchain-data-structure has led to the development of different versions of the blockchain.[6] As already explained in Step 23, combining different restrictions concerning the right to read data in the blockchain led to private and public blockchains, while restrictions on the right to write data into the blockchain led to the emergence of permissionless and permissioned blockchains. The emergence of four

---

[3]Croman, Kyle, et al. On scaling decentralized blockchains. In *Proceedings of the 3rd workshop on Bitcoin and Blockchain Research*. 2016. https://www.researchgate.net/publication/292782219_On_Scaling_Decentralized_Blockchains_A_Position_Paper; Buterin, Vitalik, Jeff Coleman, and Matthew Wampler-Doty. Notes on scalable blockchain protocols (verson 0.3). 2015. https://pdfs.semanticscholar.org/ae5b/c3aaf0e02a42f4cd41916072c87db0e04ac6.pdf?_ga=1.234210142.1100460187.1484935336.

[4]Poon, Joseph, and Thaddeus Dryja. The bitcoin lightning network: Scalable off-chain instant payments. Technical Report (draft). 2015. https://lightning.network.

[5]Tremback, Jehan, and Zack Hess. Universal payment channels. 2015. http://altheamesh.com/documents/universal-payment-channels.pdf.

[6]BitFury Group. Public versus private blockchains: Part 1, Permissioned blockchains. White paper. 2015; BitFury Group. Public versus private blockchains: Part 2, Permissionless blockchains. White paper. 2015.

different types of blockchains can be seen as a conceptual advancement as they have an impact on major characteristics of the blockchain such as its purpose, distributed nature, and architecture.

Privacy

The openness of public blockchains has already been the subject of discussions and further development since it conflicts with the level of privacy required in some application contexts. Private blockchains restrict reading access and as a result can no longer be used by everyone to clarify ownership based on the history of transaction data. Alternative approaches of protecting privacy are privacy overlays over existing blockchains[7] or distributed computing platforms that focus specifically on privacy.[8] Another approach is zero knowledge proofs, which allows you to prove the correctness of statements (e.g., statements about the current owner of a digital good) without having full access to the data on which the proof is created.[9] Regarding the blockchain, this technology could allow everyone to prove ownership-related statements without having read access to all details of transaction data.[10]

Consensus

A core element of the blockchain is its approach to select one version of the transaction history in an ongoing fashion on which all nodes consistently agree. The proof of work that causes computational costs provides the basis for the criterion that is used to choose a transaction history and to resolve conflicts between competing versions of the past. However, choosing a transaction history based on the computational power that was invested to create it left many computer scientists unsatisfied since huge computational power could be conquered and accumulated by a single organization that as a result could influence the consensus at its will.

---

[7]Meiklejohn, Sarah, and Claudio Orlandi. Privacy-enhancing overlays in bitcoin. *International Conference on Financial Cryptography and Data Security.* Berlin Heidelberg: Springer, 2015.
[8]Zyskind, Guy, Oz Nathan, and Alex Pentland. Enigma: Decentralized computation platform with guaranteed privacy. 2015. arXiv preprint arXiv:1506.03471.
[9]Krantz, Steven G. Zero knowledge proofs. July 2007. AIM Preprint Series, Volume 10-46.
[10]Miers, Ian, et al. Zerocoin: Anonymous distributed e-cash from bitcoin. In *Proceedings of the IEEE Symposium on Security and Privacy.* 2013. Washington, DC, May 19–22, 2013, pp. 397–411

Hence, different criteria as well as different algorithms for finding consensus in distributed systems have been developed and discussed. Proof of stake[11] and proof of stake velocity[12] are consensus criteria that may work well for cryptocurrencies since they tie voting power to the possession or turnover of that good that is managed by the consensus itself. Completely different algorithms for finding consensus are Paxos[13] and Raft.[14] They were developed long before the emergence of the blockchain. However, explaining Raft or Paxos at a satisfactory level is a challenge in its own right, which is beyond the scope of this book. A major challenge with alternative consensus mechanisms is that they are often conceptually more complex and thereby more difficult to prove formally. If there is a game theoretic flaw in them, it could allow corruption of the blockchain using it, and as a consequence destroy confidence in that blockchain.

Transactions

Transactions are a means to transfer ownership from one account to another and serve as a way to describe and verify ownership. It turns out that transactions are actually tiny self-contained contracts. They contain all of the necessary information to make a transfer of ownership happen. That insight led to the development of smart contracts that are executed by the blockchain. Similar to transaction data, smart contracts are machine-readable descriptions of the will of the involved parties. But unlike simple transaction data, smart contracts are much more flexible regarding the objects, subjects, actions, and conditions that can be used to describe the desired transfer of ownership. From a technical point of view, smart contracts are self-contained computer programs written in a blockchain-specific programming language. In order to accommodate smart contracts, the blockchain technology has been extended by the capability to execute programming code. This extension has transformed the blockchain from a distributed system that mainly focuses on storing transaction data into a distributed system of virtual machines that executes smart contracts.[15]

---

[11]King, Sunny, and Scott Nadal. Ppcoin: Peer-to-peer crypto-currency with proof-of-stake. Self-published paper. August 19, 2012.

[12]Ren, Larry. Proof of stake velocity: Building the social currency of the digital age. Self-published white paper. 2014.

[13]Lamport, Leslie. The part-time parliament. ACM *Transactions on Computer Systems (TOCS)* 16.2 (1998): 133–169.

[14]Ongaro, Diego, and John Ousterhout. In search of an understandable consensus algorithm. In *Proceeding of 2014 USENIX Annual Technical Conference* (USENIX ATC 14). 2014.

[15]Buterin, Vitalik. A next-generation smart contract and decentralized application platform. White paper. 2014.

The ability to run program code has opened up the possibilities for application development on the blockchain instead of just maintaining simple transaction data. When talking about smart contracts, we need to be careful; although the term initially implied a contract between counterparties, it is now used to refer to a piece of code that is managed and executed in an appropriated blockchain. However, there are moves from the legal profession to develop something more akin to that initial idea based on the idea of Ricardian contracts.[16]

Due to their flexibility, smart contracts can be used to describe a wide range of real-world contracts such as paying rent on a regular basis, taking out a loan, repaying a loan, placing and settling complex bets, and issuing insurance payments on the occurrence of damages or complex events. As a result, the smart contract is the most important and promising development of the blockchain in the past few years.

Inventory Data

The initial blockchain as discussed in the preceding steps is concerned with maintaining the integrity of an immutable append-only data store that can be used among others for maintaining the whole history of transaction data. However, as discussed in Step 9, ownership can be managed based on both transaction data and inventory data. The former approach seems to be appropriate when managing simple data, while the latter has proven useful in the context of smart contracts where the whole system is often considered a collection of states that can include arbitrary information such as account balances, bets, insurance contracts, reputation, or data that represent objects in the physical world.[17] As a result, the state of the whole system is stored as inventory data and is transformed by the execution of smart contracts, which are stored separately in an immutable append-only data store.

Data Structure

The blockchain-data-structure is not a straight line of blocks; instead, it is actually a tree-shaped data structure whose branches represent conflicting versions of the history of transaction data. The major challenge of the blockchain-algorithm is to let the nodes of the distributed system select one of the branches as the authoritative chain consistently. An alternative approach of storing transaction data is to utilize a directed acyclic graph of blocks instead

[16]Grigg, Ian. The Ricardian contract. 2004. In *Proceedings of the 1st IEEE International Workshop on Electronic Contracting*. IEEE, 2004: 25–31.
[17]Wood, Gavin. Ethereum: A secure decentralized generalized transaction ledger. 2014. http://gavwood.com/paper.pdf.

of a tree-shaped data structure. One can imagine a directed acyclic graph of blocks as a tree-shaped blockchain-data-structure whose branches merge later on. The usage of an acyclic graph for storing the transaction history has far-reaching consequences on performance, clarifying ownership, and reaching consensus among peers.[18]

Major Accomplishments of the Blockchain

It is well-accepted knowledge that people tend to overestimate the short-term effects of technology while ignoring its long-term impacts. The evolution of the Internet and its impact on our society not only confirm that wisdom, but it also shows that estimating long-term effects of technical innovations is hard. However, the following aspects are promising candidates for becoming the long-term accomplishments of the blockchain:

- Disintermediation

- Automation

- Standardization

- Streamlining processes

- Increased processing speed

- Cost reduction

- Shift toward trust in protocols and technology

- Making trust a commodity

- Increased technology awareness

Disintermediation

The blockchain does not destroy the role of the middleman but instead it establishes itself as a digital and strictly rule-following middleman. Replacing one middleman with another may not be a big deal, but replacing a human organization that relies on the trust of its customers with a software system that encodes trust is a huge achievement. Furthermore, replacing a cascade of middlemen with one system that orchestrates the direct interactions of peers in a secure way is indeed a huge achievement. Hence, disintermediation is an accomplishment of the blockchain whose impact could remain.

---

[18]Lewenberg, Yoad, Yonatan Sompolinsky, and Aviv Zohar. Inclusive block chain protocols. In *International Conference on Financial Cryptography and Data Security* Berlin Heidelberg: Springer, 2015.

Automation

In order to fulfill its role as digital middleman, the blockchain relies on automation. The more the blockchain is used, the more it will replace manual tasks of established intermediaries by automated interactions between peers. Hence, another accomplishment of the blockchain could its potential to foster automation.

Standardization

The automated processing of transactions offered by the blockchain is based on the existence of rules and standards. Hence, the more the blockchain is used, the more transactions and interactions between contracting parties will be standardized. So fostering standardization of peer interactions could be another long-term accomplishment of the blockchain.

Streamlining Processes

As a consequence of standardization and automation, business processes will become more transparent and streamlined. Many organizations reviewed and analyzed their business processes as a side effect of preparing themselves for transition to the blockchain. Hence, the review of existing business processes and redesigning and streamlining them could be another accomplishment of the blockchain that may persist.

Increased Processing Speed

Disintermediation, standardization, streamlined processes, and automation lead to a significant speed up of processes. Hence, one can expect that the more the blockchain is used, the more timely transactions and interactions between contracting parties will be executed. The speeding up of processes that once involved time-consuming manually performed tasks could be another long-term contribution of the blockchain.

Cost Reduction

The economic consequence of automation, disintermediation, and standardization is often a reduction of costs. History has shown that cost-reducing effects of automation have driven and reshaped many industries and as a result made many goods affordable to a wider range of people. However, the cost-reducing effect of automation is not limited to producing cars, televisions, mobile phones, and clothes. The cost-reduction of intermediation could be the most noticeable long-term contribution of the blockchain from an economic point of view.

Shift Toward Trust in Protocols and Technology

The blockchain replaces trust in humans or human organizations with the trust in the unerring logic of computer-based verification and the power of consensus. This may change our perception of trust and reliability on the individual level as well as on the level of the society. Hence, the shift toward trust in security protocols and computationally attained consensus may be regarded as one of the most important long-term effects of the blockchain from a sociological point of view.

Making Trust a Commodity

Automation and standardization did not only reduce production time and costs in many industries but also made many consumer goods that were expensive in the past affordable for a huge number of people. For example, can you remember how expensive a pocket calculator, a PC, or a mobile phone was 30 years ago? Nowadays, pocket calculators are given away as marketing goodies, and computers with magnitudes more power than the computers used in the first NASA space programs are affordable on a pocket change budget. This is mainly due to the automation and standardization in the production of computer chips and semiconductors. We can expect that trust and secure initiation, execution, and settlement of business interactions will become as inexpensive and ubiquitously available as pocket calculators due to the automation and standardization introduced by the blockchain. This could be the most visible long-term impact of the blockchain for those who need to initiate, execute, and settle business interactions every day as part of their daily business.

Increased Technology Awareness

The blockchain is a technical construct of high complexity that solves the highly technical problem of achieving integrity in distributed peer-to-peer systems by using immutable data structures and a consensus algorithm. This topic does not seem to be predestined to attract the attention of the business world. However, the blockchain has received and continues to receive a lot of attention from many sides. The increased interest in technology and the rising awareness about the role of technology in our lives may be regarded as side effects of the blockchain, but they are welcome developments since the success of many industries as well as the wealth of our society critically depend on mastering technological challenges.

Possible Disadvantages

Besides its positive effects and accomplishments, the blockchain can also cause unwanted side effects or even negative outcomes. The most important ones are:

- Lack of privacy
- Loss of personal responsibility
- Loss of jobs
- Reintermediation

Lack of Privacy

Public blockchains do not hide any of their data. Instead, everyone is able to read the whole history of transactions. This level of transparency is frightening for those who want to protect their privacy. These concerns are understandable when taking into account the level at which personal data are already collected and utilized by large corporations or intelligence agencies. However, this criticism may foster the development and spread of private blockchains or the utilization of advanced security protocols. Additionally, this could initiate the idea that people could own their personal data and be able to sell the right to access or use it. As a result, intermediaries such as established providers of search engines and social media platforms may lose user acceptance and market share.

Loss of Responsibility

Loss of personal responsibility is often considered a consequence of disintermediation. Intermediaries not only bring different parties of a contract together but may also provide guarantees. They offer reconciliation in cases when transactions do not work out as intended, and they are also obliged to take responsibility for their actions. The shift from trust in people and human organizations toward trust in protocols and technology may lead to a loss of personal service and personal responsibility in the context of initiating, executing, and settling contractual interactions. Due to open questions regarding the legal acceptance of the blockchain, people expressed their doubt whether the blockchain as a fully automated protocol-driven transaction machinery can take the responsibility of its actions in the same way traditional intermediaries do. However, this criticism may foster legal initiatives for clarifying open issues regarding the legal status of the blockchain.

Loss of Jobs

Automation and standardization have not only shaped the process and the costs of producing goods but also caused friction in the labor market. Many players in the financial industry such as banks, brokers, custodians, money-transfer agencies, and notaries are directly tied to their roles as intermediaries. Many jobs in these institutions could be at risk when a huge portion of financial transactions are processed in an automated fashion through the blockchain.

Reintermediation

The complexity and its open legal status may discourage individual people as well as organizations from using the blockchain, which can cause an effect that counteracts disintermediation. Instead of using the blockchain in order to interact with contracting parties directly, people may decide to utilize services offered by intermediaries, which in turn use the blockchain. This could lead to a renaissance of intermediaries that are supposed to be replaced by the blockchain. This effect could seriously slow down the adoption of the blockchain and counteract some of its major accomplishments.

The Future

Predicting the future is not an easy task, in particular when considering a new technology that is the object of active research and further development. However, one can identify some indications that point to a likely future scenario. In particular, it seems that public permissionless blockchains have a limited commercial use due to their limited scalability and lack or privacy. On the other hand, it seems that private permissioned blockchains are those that attract the most attention from the business side. As a result, we may see the following developments in the future:

- Limited enthusiast projects
- Large-scale commercial usage
- Governmental projects

Limited Enthusiast Projects

Limited enthusiast projects may utilize public permissionless blockchains and are most likely to be initiated and supported by blockchain enthusiasts and blockchain purists who are motivated by the complete openness and the purely distributed nature of the system. The supporters of those projects may regard their engagement as a political statement or commitment to alternative software systems that absolves them from any kind of governmental or commercial control and coordination. Cryptocurrencies as alternative money that is supposed to be independent of governmental regulation as well as independent reputation systems or systems for managing identity independently from governmental identity documents might be a major application case in that context.

Large-Scale Commercial Usage

Large-scale commercial blockchain projects are expected to utilize private permissioned blockchains. These projects will most likely be initiated and run by consortiums of leading companies of a certain sector or industry. Realizing the gains of standardization, automation, process streamlining, and cost reduction will be the major reason for supporting those projects. These projects may also be based on the idea of finding a compromise that allows the participants to utilize the advantages of the blockchain without making themselves dispensable due to disintermediation. It could be possible that each major sector such as banking, financial exchanges, insurance, health care, payments, and retail will develop and offer their own sector-wide blockchain solution.

Governmental Projects

As governmental projects, these blockchain ventures are tax funded and therefore free from most commercial restrictions that influence blockchain projects in the private sector. These projects may be initiated and run as part of e-government initiatives that aim to digitalize manual processes or to replace legacy infrastructure. Taxation, monitoring, digital identity, record management, or monetary policy could benefit from the properties of the blockchain. However, open legal questions as well as existing data security and privacy laws may significantly limit the benefit of the blockchain within the public sector.

Outlook

This step finished and rounded off this intellectual journey toward an understanding of the blockchain. After highlighting areas of research and further development of the blockchain, this step mentioned some of its alternatives and possible long-term accomplishments, disadvantages, and future usages. The history of the Internet has taught us not only how volatile and unpredictable but also how challenging and rewarding the usage and the development of a new technology can be. Whatever the future of the blockchain will be, we can decide to be not just witnesses but also active participants of an exciting and challenging technological transition that has the potential to be one of the biggest things since the invention of the Internet.

Summary

- The blockchain has been and will continue to be the subject of further improvements and developments such as variations in its implementation, improving efficiency, improving scalability, and conceptual advances.

- Smart contracts, zero-knowledge proofs, and alternative ways to achieve consensus are major areas of conceptual advancement of the blockchain.

- Besides it technical merits, the blockchain may be honored for the following long-term accomplishments:

  - Disintermediation

  - Automation

  - Standardization

  - Streamlining processes

  - Increased processing speed

  - Cost reduction

  - Shift toward trust in protocols and technology

  - Making trust a commodity

  - Increased technology awareness

- Possible disadvantages of the blockchain are:

  - Lack of privacy

  - Loss of personal responsibility

  - Loss of jobs

  - Reintermediation

- Possible usages of the blockchain to be seen in the future are:

  - Limited enthusiast projects

  - Large-scale commercial projects

  - Governmental projects

I

Index

A

Algorithm, 34

All-or-nothing approach, 138

Application layer, 4–5, 10
  functional aspects
    clarifying ownership, 192
    transferring ownership, 192
  nonfunctional aspects
    availability, 193
    censorship proof, 193
    open, 193
    pseudoanonymous, 193
    reliable, 193

Asymmetric cryptography, 190
  authorize transactions, 100
  complementary keys, 96
  create and distribute keys, 98
  decrypt cypher text, 97
  identify users, 99
  private to public, 99
  public to private, 99
  schematic illustration, 97

Auditing, 227

Authentication, 43–44

Authoritative chain, 168, 174–177

Authorization, 43–44, 68

Automation, 243

B

Bakery, 183

Bank account, 21

Bank notes, 50

Beaten paths, 165, 167

Behavioral integrity, 6

Bitcoin system, 187

Black key, 97

Block, 34, 160
  hash, 120
  header, 139, 156
    reference, 130–131

Blockchain
  -algorithm
    competition, 157–158
    identical working rhythm, 159
    metaphor used, 191
    peer control, 158
    punishment, 157
    purpose, 191
    reward, 156
    validation rules, 156
  -data-structure
    block header reference, 130–131
    book, 113
    comparison, 118
    content, 115, 120
    content reference numbers, 120
    get rid of spine, 117
    intended *vs.* unintended changes, 132
    mental unit, 119
    Merkle root, 129–130
    Merkle tree, 128
    metaphor used, 191
    new transactions, 125–126
    ordering catalog, 119

D. Drescher, *Blockchain Basics*, DOI 10.1007/978-1-4842-2604-9

Get the eBook for only $4.99!

Why limit yourself?

Now you can take the weightless companion with you wherever you go and access your content on your PC, phone, tablet, or reader.

Since you've purchased this print book, we are happy to offer you the eBook for just $4.99.

Convenient and fully searchable, the PDF version enables you to easily find and copy code—or perform examples by quickly toggling between instructions and applications.

To learn more, go to http://www.apress.com/us/shop/companion or contact support@apress.com.

Made in the USA
Middletown, DE
25 October 2018